FREE COUNTRY

Free Country
Selected Lectures and Talks

Sydney Kentridge QC

·HART·
PUBLISHING
OXFORD AND PORTLAND, OREGON
2012

Published in the United Kingdom by Hart Publishing Ltd
16C Worcester Place, Oxford, OX1 2JW
Telephone: +44 (0)1865 517530
Fax: +44 (0)1865 510710
E-mail: mail@hartpub.co.uk
Website: http://www.hartpub.co.uk

Published in North America (US and Canada) by
Hart Publishing
c/o International Specialized Book Services
920 NE 58th Avenue, Suite 300
Portland, OR 97213-3786
USA
Tel: +1 503 287 3093 or toll-free: (1) 800 944 6190
Fax: +1 503 280 8832
E-mail: orders@isbs.com
Website: http://www.isbs.com

British Library Cataloguing in Publication Data
Data Available

ISBN: 978-1-84946-467-3

Typeset by Forewords Ltd, Oxford
Printed and bound in Great Britain by
TJ International Ltd, Padstow, Cornwall

Foreword

Sydney Kentridge QC has long been admired within the English-speaking legal professions as a brilliant advocate, an outstanding lawyer and, during the apartheid years in South Africa, a courageous defender of the individual against an oppressive state. His advocacy at the inquest of Steve Biko came to the attention of a wider audience when he was portrayed on stage and screen by Albert Finney. In 1977, the same year as the Biko inquest, Sydney was called to the Bar of England and Wales and joined chambers at 1 Brick Court (now Brick Court Chambers) in London. Since then, he has pursued a second, equally celebrated, career in this country, appearing in many of the leading cases in the fields of commercial and public law. He was not forgotten in South Africa. When apartheid was abolished and a new Constitutional Court was established in 1994, Sydney served on the new Court as an Acting Justice and delivered its first judgment. In 1999 he was knighted 'for services to international law and justice'. And when, to mark that occasion, the Bar of England and Wales held a dinner at the Banqueting House, Whitehall, in his honour, Lord Alexander of Weedon QC was able to say, without any exaggeration, that, if the timing had been different, Sydney would surely have been Chief Justice of South Africa and, had he come to England earlier, he would surely have become a Law Lord. 'As it is,' Lord Alexander added, 'he is simply the most highly regarded advocate in the Commonwealth.'

As colleagues in Brick Court Chambers for many years, we were lucky enough to work on cases with Sydney and to observe the genius of his advocacy at first hand. We were also able to attend talks or lectures that he gave in the Inns of Court and elsewhere. Some of these, such as the Sir David Williams Lecture and the FA Mann Lecture, were prestigious public lectures which were published at the time in legal journals. Another, on the ethics of advocacy, was published privately by the South Eastern Circuit and distributed to all its members. Others survived only in Sydney's notes and in the memories of his audiences.

It occurred to us that these lectures ought to be collected so that they can be appreciated by a wider audience and for the benefit of posterity. Many of them are, we believe, not only of historical importance but timeless in their relevance and appeal.

With some diffidence we approached Sydney with the suggestion and offered to assist in the editing. To our delight, he agreed 'to see what he could find at home' and to re-read his published and unpublished manuscripts to consider if any would pass muster. However, he proved to be a merciless critic of his own work, and our combined powers of advocacy proved totally inadequate to redeem some of the material from the outer darkness to which he decided to consign it. The result of this winnowing is the collection of twelve lectures and talks which appear in this volume.

The lectures span a period of more than thirty years, from 1979 to 2011. With the exception of the last, they are reproduced (with minor editing) in the order that they were originally given. The lectures cover a range of topics, but also contain some common themes.

The first four lectures were all delivered during the years of apartheid in South Africa. They describe some of the laws which not merely permitted but required racial discrimination in a way that is without any parallel elsewhere; and they relate how civil liberties and the protections essential for a fair trial were undermined, in particular by the Terrorism Act. The lectures provide a vivid reminder of the injustice of that system, from the perspective of an advocate who practised under it. But what makes that experience of special fascination is that the rule of law in South Africa, although distorted, was never completely destroyed. If the right to be represented by independent counsel had been abolished or if every treason trial had ended in conviction, there would have been no role left for the advocate. But, as Sydney explains, that was never the case. Even in the darkest hours, those accused of treason and other political crimes continued to be represented in court, and were sometimes acquitted. Out of Sydney's experience of practising in those circumstances emerge two themes which run through this volume: on the one hand, an acute sense of the fragility of the rights and values that define a free country; and on the other hand, and at the same time, an intense appreciation of just how much such rights and freedoms, which we may sometimes take for granted, really matter.

The outlook of these lectures changes over time. The first lecture—*The Pathology of a Legal System*, given in Philadelphia in 1979—is deeply pessimistic and ends on a grim note. Yet by the time Sydney came to give the John Foster Lecture, *Civil*

Rights in Southern Africa: The Prospect for the Future, in 1986, his prognosis had become less bleak. His forecast that, by the end of the century, there would be a peaceful transfer of power in South Africa and agreement on an entrenched constitutional bill of rights was prescient and mistaken (happily) only as to the timing.

Every barrister has been asked the question: how can you defend a client whom you know is guilty? Even though the question in that stark form in practice seldom arises (and admits of an easy answer), related questions give rise to real moral difficulty. How can it be honourable to present a case in which you do not believe, or to defend a cause or conduct which you think reprehensible, or to impugn the honesty of a witness who is in all probability telling the truth? These are the questions discussed in *The Ethics of Advocacy*. It is a lecture which anyone who has been troubled by such questions, or who has practised as an advocate without being troubled by them, should read.

In *Freedom of Speech: Is it the Primary Right?*, Sydney discusses the ever topical issue of whether the right to freedom of speech should prevail over other rights with which it may conflict, such as the right to reputation or the right to a fair trial. He begins his answer to that question in what is surely the right place by considering just why it is that we value freedom of speech.

A Judge's Duty in a Revolution tells the story of a case which tested the resolve of the Queen's judges to uphold the constitution after the government unlawfully claimed to have abolished it. The case was brought by Mrs Madzimbamuto, whom Sydney represented, against the Minister of Justice in Southern Rhodesia (as it then was) after the Smith government had unilaterally declared independence from the UK. Although the setting of the case has passed into history, the issues which it raised and Sydney's disquieting account of how the judges responded to the challenges they faced are of universal concern and interest.

As the *Madzimbamuto* case shows, the independence and quality of the judiciary cannot be presumed. In *The Highest Court: Selecting the Judges*, Sydney brings the wisdom of his experience to bear in discussing how judges should be selected to sit in the highest court in the UK.

The UK has faced its own challenges to civil liberties in the last decade arising out of the threat of terrorism. In *Taking Liberties*, an address given to the Bar Conference in 2007, Sydney considers whether a proper balance has been struck between the protection of public safety and the protection of liberty. This is also one of the issues explored in *The Rule of Law: Ideals and Realities*, a talk given to the Commonwealth Law Conference.

The last two lectures return to Sydney's experiences of practising in South Africa in the time of apartheid. In the Steve Biko Memorial Lecture, *Evil under the Sun*, delivered in 2011, Sydney has given for the first time his own account of Steve Biko's death. The story is a shocking one which has been told before, but never better. The final lecture, *A Barrister in the Apartheid Years*, describes some other extraordinary cases in which Sydney appeared in South Africa during those years. Of the political activists whom he represented, he mentions three in particular: Chief Albert Luthuli, who was the President of the African National Congress in the 1950s, Nelson Mandela and Archbishop Desmond Tutu. That leads him to observe, 'without false or any other modesty', that he has one distinction which he doubts that any other advocate can claim: all those three clients were winners of the Nobel Peace Prize. It seems unlikely that any other advocate will ever attain that distinction.

In *The Ethics of Advocacy* Sydney advises his audience that 'in the end your advocacy will be a reflection of your own character and personality, and your own particular talents'. One of the great pleasures of this collection is that the author's voice and personality, including his understated sense of humour, are evident throughout. His is not just the voice of a great advocate; it is also wise and humane.

Today is Sydney's 90th birthday. However, for Sydney, it is business as usual, as he is briefed to appear today in the Supreme Court of the United Kingdom. We wish him many happy returns of the day.

David Lloyd Jones
George Leggatt
5 November 2012

Preface

When, after nearly 30 years at the Johannesburg Bar, I was called to the English Bar by Lincoln's Inn, one of my sponsors, Sir Michael Kerr, suggested that I apply for a tenancy at 1 Brick Court in the Temple. I was duly interviewed by Bob Alexander QC, who was de facto head of Chambers, and Ron Burley, its formidable chief clerk. I was taken on provisionally as a 'door tenant' and in due course as a real tenant, with a room and a desk of my own. I do not think that Bob and Burley consulted anyone else in Chambers. Those were more easygoing days. At all events, their acceptance of my rather diffident application was a stroke of good fortune of which I have been constantly aware.

Over more than 30 years my fellow barristers at Brick Court Chambers have given me support, friendship and many kindnesses. The latest of these was the proposal by two of them that some of the lectures and talks I have given over the years be published, and that they would take on the burden of helping me to select the material for publication and of editing it. No longer members of Chambers, they are now Lord Justice David Lloyd Jones and Mr Justice George Leggatt. I am most grateful to them not only for their very generous introduction but also for their much-needed editorial firmness. I am also grateful to the publishers for taking on the book and for their expedition in producing it.

The lectures which follow have little claim to scholarship. Some of them were informal talks rather than lectures. For the most part they simply reflect some of the concerns which arose out of my work as an advocate in both England and South Africa. Those which relate to South Africa under apartheid may still, I hope, have some historical interest.

If these twelve pieces seem to be a meagre product of a very long professional life, I can only respond that it is the nature of the work of a barrister that it leaves no memorials of either its successes or (more fortunately) its disasters.

SYDNEY KENTRIDGE
November, 2012

Contents

~

1

The Pathology of a Legal System: Criminal Justice in South Africa*

~

A SURPRISINGLY LARGE number of American lawyers visit South Africa or follow closely what is happening in that country. Their fascination with the legal institutions of a small and distant country, whose common law is the Roman-Dutch law, has often struck me as remarkable. I do not complain of it, as one of its agreeable consequences (from my point of view, at least) is that I have been invited to give this lecture. Part of the explanation, no doubt, is that the courts in South Africa deal with laws and institutions that bear an uncomfortably close resemblance to those with which American courts had to deal in the fairly recent past – laws and institutions that permit or even ordain discrimination on grounds of race and colour. Perhaps a more profound reason for American attention to South Africa is that South Africa exemplifies in the most intense form what is possibly the major international issue of the second half of the twentieth century – namely, the correlation between skin colour and enjoyment of political power, civil liberty, and economic affluence. Attention is focused on South Africa not because it has quantitatively less freedom, less justice, or less democratic government than a hundred other countries one could name. Those goods do exist in South Africa, but they are strictly rationed on the sole basis of colour – not on citizenship or birth or merit, but colour alone. Discrimination on the ground of colour in South Africa is not an aberration to be deprecated and remedied, but an

* This was the Owen J Roberts Memorial Lecture, delivered 18 October 1979 at the University of Pennsylvania Law School.

institution that is authorised and, frequently, actually commanded by statute. That is the essential difference from the discrimination that undoubtedly continues to be found in the United States, in England, or in New Zealand. It is not discrimination but integration that is expressly forbidden by the Parliament of South Africa.

At the time when *Brown v Board of Education*[1] was before the United States Supreme Court, and the doctrine of 'separate but equal' was on the point of disappearing from American jurisprudence, the same doctrine, which had been blessed twenty years earlier by South Africa's highest court,[2] was also disappearing from South African law. It was, however, disappearing in a different direction. A short statute, known as the Reservation of Separate Amenities Act 1953, simply and clearly provided not merely that public premises or public vehicles would be set apart or reserved for the exclusive use of persons belonging to a particular race or class (section 2), but also that any such setting apart or reservation would not be invalid on the ground that the premises or vehicles reserved for the use of one class were not equal to those reserved for any other race or class (section 3).

Another aspect of the South African system makes it a particular subject of interested observation by lawyers in Western countries. Notwithstanding statutes such as that I have just mentioned, and notwithstanding the increasingly authoritarian tone of government in South Africa, the traditional forms of legal process have not been abandoned. Trials, including trials of enemies or critics of the government (two categories which those in high levels of government often have difficulty distinguishing), take place in ordinary courts, open to the press and usually to the public, before the ordinary judges of the land. The accused are entitled to be defended by counsel, and there are always counsel willing to defend them. For many years (and for good reasons into which I need not enter here), we have had no jury trials in South Africa. The judge himself is the trier of fact. Save for this feature, however, a criminal trial in South Africa, up to very recent times at least, was conducted subject to those rules of evidence and procedure that, with the English language and the game of cricket, have been the most beneficent and lasting legacies of the British Empire.

But in very recent times, under the stress of sharpened conflict

---

[1] 347 US 433 (1954).
[2] *Minister of Posts & Telegraphs v Rasool* 1934 AD 167.

between the rulers and the ruled that has gone hand in hand with the increasingly authoritarian tone of government to which I have referred, we have witnessed – or, some of us, experienced – a profound distortion of our traditional legal system. A distortion, but not a disappearance. So there is something to be observed, by ourselves as South African lawyers, as well as by foreign lawyers who have a fundamentally similar conception of what constitutes a fair trial: the pathology of a system of criminal justice. This applies largely, although not entirely, to political trials, that is, prosecutions for political offences. It is this pathological condition to which I shall devote most of this lecture. I shall describe it, attempt to define the 'philosophy' underlying this departure from previously accepted norms of proper judicial process, and finally say a word about those who participate in it, both judges and lawyers.

There are two preliminary observations to be made. First, by reason of the similarity between the American system and the South African system, one may take this to be an implicit exercise in comparative criminal procedure. Comparative studies, especially in this field, tend to contain a strong moral element, sometimes disquieting but to American lawyers, no doubt, usually satisfying. The procedural novelties – to use a neutral term – that I shall describe have been created not by the judges, but by a sovereign legislature that is unfettered by any such eighteenth-century institution as a bill of rights. Americans may understandably take comfort in the fact that their Constitution, as presently interpreted, does not permit such things to happen. In many Western countries, including the United States, however, there are persons in powerful positions who maintain that existing forms of criminal procedure are weighted too heavily in favour of the accused, and that politically motivated crimes in particular call for special forms of procedure making it easier to obtain convictions. An examination of what may happen to a legal system when these views prevail may therefore be of some general interest.

The second preliminary observation to be made concerns the legitimacy of the criticism of the South African system of political trials. The South African government justifies its security legislation, including those criminal procedure statutes to which I shall refer, on the ground that South Africa faces a serious threat of subversion from within and outside its borders. The existence of this threat may be fully accepted. Persons charged with political

offences in South Africa have often been shown to have been
engaged in activities that in any country would be regarded as
criminal, activities involving actual or potential violence against
the state. The question remains, however, whether this unde-
niable fact justifies the forms of procedure under which those
charged with such offences are now tried.

Further, much as the South African government resents criticisms of its laws and practices, it has in a sense invited them. For
the South African government firmly maintains that it is a part
of the free world and that it is indeed the main, if not the sole,
representative in Africa of western civilization. The distinguished
and perceptive judge in whose honour this lecture is presented, in
a celebrated address given at Oxford, referred to the rule of law
as an idea recognised by what he called 'highly civilised nations'.
Asked what countries he would include in this category, Justice
Roberts replied:

> My test would be, first, a country that has a representative form of
> government; second, a country where individual liberty and freedom
> are protected by law; [and third], where there are bounds and limits
> to what the government can do to an individual.[3]

As a South African lawyer, that is the criterion by which I would
want my legal system to be judged. I am not impressed when I
am told that things are done worse in the USSR or Uganda, or,
for that matter, in the Comoro Islands. In South Africa we are the
inheritors of two of the great legal systems of the world, the Roman-
Dutch law of Holland and the common law of England. We should
invite and accept judgment by the standards of those systems.

I. CRIMINAL PROCEDURE IN SOUTH AFRICA

A. The Traditional Standards

In order to understand the pathology of a body, one must know
something of its normal functions. It is not necessary for me to
describe at length the normal rules of South African criminal
procedure, as most of its features will be exceedingly familiar.
First the rules relating to arrest, with or without warrant, are

---

[3] Discussion by Justice Owen J Roberts at Oxford following his lecture, 'The Rule
of Law in the International Community' (1951), quoted in AL Goodhart, 'The Rule of
Law and Absolute Sovereignty' (1958) 106 *University of Pennsylvania Law Review* 943.

similar in general to those of American law. The arrested person has the right to remain silent and must be warned by the police that he has this right before he is interrogated. He has a right to consult a legal adviser immediately after he has been arrested. He must be brought before a court within forty-eight hours of his arrest. He may apply for bail. Even before the process in court commences, he has (or had in the past) the broad protection of the writ of habeas corpus, or its Roman-Dutch equivalent, the writ *de homine libero exhibendo*.[4] His trial is an adversary proceeding in which he is protected by the privilege against self-incrimination and in which the burden of proof rests upon the prosecution. He has the right to counsel of his choice (subject, admittedly, to paying the going fee or to finding someone else willing to pay it) and, in general, the right to be confronted with the witnesses against him. The rule against hearsay evidence applies with full, some would even say outmoded, rigour. And no confession is admissible against him that was not in all respects freely and voluntarily made.

Of course, as in all systems, these rules have not always been observed. Confessions made under physical or mental duress do slip past judicial scrutiny; often the requisite police warning of the right to be silent is not given; various statutes alter the burden of proof; the accused cannot always afford counsel, especially the black accused who, in an average year, constitute ninety per cent of all criminal defendants.[5] Nonetheless, these rules, some statutory and some judge-made, have set a standard of due process, the standard by which the fairness of a trial ought to be judged.

The time has now come to examine to what extent these standards still apply in South Africa to trials or political offences. I do not pause to define minutely what is meant by a political offence. It has sometimes been disputed in South Africa, as it has else-

---

[4] See J Voet, *The Selective Voet, Being the Commentary on the Pandects* (Gane's Translation) 528–29; S Kentridge, 'Habeas Corpus Procedure in South Africa' (1962) 79 *South African Law Journal* 283, 285. In the Roman-Dutch law, the approach to this writ is entirely without technicality. As stated by one South African judge, the rule is simply that every arrest is prima facie unlawful and must be justified in court by the arresting authority if called upon to do so: *Principal Immigration Officer v Narayansamy* 1916 TPD 274, 276 (quoting the unreported opinion of Wessels J in the court below). See also the powerful opinion of Rumpff CJ in *Wood v Ondangwa Tribal Auth* 1975 (2) SA 294 (A), 310–11, in which the Appellate Division (South Africa's final appeals court) reemphasised that the remedy should be construed as broadly as possible.

[5] See, eg South Africa Institute of Race Relations, *A Survey of Race Relations in South Africa* (1978) 66.

where, whether such offences exist. It is enough to say that I am referring to crimes committed with the political motive of altering or protesting against the current political dispensation.

South Africa has had an interesting – some would say an over-interesting – history of political turbulence, which has been marked by many series of political trials, including trials for high treason. During the Anglo-Boer War, many Boers living in the British colonies of the Cape of Good Hope and Natal assisted the Boer forces; in 1914 some thousands of diehard veterans of the Anglo-Boer War went into rebellion against the government of what was then the Union of South Africa; in 1922 there was a revolt of white workers on the Witwatersrand; and from 1939 to 1945 a number of Afrikaner nationalists acted in support of the German cause. All these events resulted in trials for treason. In 1958, thirty leaders of the African National Congress and its political allies were charged with conspiracy to overthrow the state by violence. The charge there too was treason. This trial differed in an important respect from previous South African treason trials in that most of the accused were black. After a trial which lasted from August 1958 to March 1961, all the accused were acquitted.[6] All these trials were conducted according to the normal rules of South African criminal procedure. Indeed, when the charge was treason, the prosecution had the added burden of complying with a provision that, up to 1977, had always been embodied in the South African Criminal Procedure Acts.[7] These Acts provided that no court would 'convict any accused of treason except upon the evidence of two witnesses where one overt act is charged, or where two or more overt acts are so charged, upon the evidence of one witness to each such overt act'.[8]

B. The Terrorism Act

Possibly because of the highly publicised failure of the prosecution in the treason trial of 1958 to 1961, possibly influenced also by

---

[6] The record of this trial is analysed in T Kabis, *The Treason Trial in South Africa* (1965).

[7] Eg Criminal Procedure Act 56 of 1955, s 256(b), repealed by Criminal Procedure Act 51 of 1977, s 208.

[8] Ibid. This provision was first enacted in England in the reign of William II in the Statute of Treasons 1695, s 2. It was repealed in England by the Treason Act 1945, and in South Africa by Criminal Procedure Act 51 of 1977, s 208. It is embodied in Art 3, s 3 of the US Constitution.

the happenings at Sharpeville in 1960,[9] as well as by disturbances in the Cape in 1962,[10] the South African government adopted a new approach to the prosecution of political offenders. After experimenting with amendments to various other statutes – all designed to facilitate the prosecution and conviction of persons alleged to be carrying on subversive activities against the state – the government, in 1967, put through Parliament an Act that introduced, under the name of 'terroristic activities' or 'terrorism', a new form of statutory treason.[11] According to this Act, a person is guilty of the offence of participating in terroristic activities if he commits any act whatsoever with the intention of endangering the maintenance of law and order in the Republic of South Africa.[12] Upon conviction he is liable to the penalties appropriate to common law treason, including the death penalty, and subject to a minimum sentence of five years' imprisonment, which may not be suspended.[13]

This Act is a considerable extension of the concept of treason. In the Roman-Dutch law, the crime of treason is limited to acts committed with the intention of overthrowing the state by violence. That element is not essential under the Terrorism Act. On the contrary, the Act, with the aid of presumptions that transfer the burden of proof to the accused, covers a range of offences going well beyond what would ordinarily be regarded as terrorism or treason. For example, the Act prohibits activities that are likely 'to cause substantial financial loss to any person or the State'.[14] Thus, if it is proved that the accused organised a strike or an economic boycott that was likely to result in such loss, then, unless he can prove beyond a reasonable doubt that that was not his intent, he must be found guilty of terrorism.

The Act's practical effect is greatly extended by the inclusion of a second class of actions that would not ordinarily be regarded as treasonable, namely, actions calculated to create feelings of hostility between the white and black inhabitants of the country.[15]

---

[9] On 21 March 1960, a crowd of some thousands of blacks gathered at the police station in Sharpeville (about thirty miles south of Johannesburg) to protest against the pass laws. The police fired on the crowd. Sixty-nine blacks were killed, and 180 were wounded.

[10] On 21 November 1972 in Paarl, a small town near Cape Town, a rioting black mob killed two whites and seriously injured three others.

[11] Terrorism Act 83 of 1967.

[12] Ibid, s 2(1).

[13] Ibid, s 2(1).

[14] Ibid, s 2(2)(h).

[15] Ibid, s 2(2)(i).

An actual case illustrates the operation of this provision. A young black man wrote a violently anti-white poem. He showed it to only one person, a seventeen-year-old girl. The publication of the poem to this girl was found to have had the likely result of causing her to feel hostile towards whites. The accused could not prove beyond reasonable doubt that he did not intend her to have such feelings. He was consequently convicted of terrorism and sentenced to five years' imprisonment.[16]

The Act contains many procedural provisions designed to assist the prosecution. The rule against documentary hearsay evidence is modified in favour of the state by an extraordinary, but much used, provision.[17] No court is permitted to grant bail to a person charged under the Act without the consent of the Attorney-General.[18] Acquittal does not preclude subsequent arraignment on another charge arising out of the same conduct.[19] Perhaps most remarkable, this statute became law on 12 June 1967, but its substantive, procedural, and evidentiary provisions are all deemed to have come into effect in June 1962.[20] That is to say, the Act was made to apply retrospectively to a time five years before it was enacted. In one leading case, the accused had actually been arrested and in custody for about a year before the Terrorism Act was passed; they were nonetheless charged and convicted under that Act.[21]

These provisions do not in themselves explain the actual working of the Terrorism Act. The key to its practical operation is to be found in section 6. This section permits the police, without judicial warrant, to detain any person who any senior police officer has reason to believe either committed an offence under the Act or has any knowledge of such an offence.[22] The object of the detention is interrogation, and the detention may continue either until the detainee has answered all questions put to him to the satisfaction of the police or until the police are convinced that 'no useful

---

[16] *S v Motsau* (WLD, unreported, April 1974).
[17] Terrorism Act 83 of 1967, s 2(3). Under this provision, the prosecutor may produce, not through a witness but from his own file, any document that on its face emanated from any organisation of which the accused was at any time a member. The document is admissible against the accused, and its contents are prima facie presumed to be true. See, eg *S v Malepane* 1979 (1) SA 1009 (W), 1015 per Le Roux J.
[18] Terrorism Act 83 of 1967, s 5(f).
[19] Ibid, s 5(h).
[20] Ibid, s 9(l).
[21] *S v Tuhadeleni* 1969 (1) SA 153.
[22] Terrorism Act 83 of 1967, s 6(1).

purpose will be served by his further detention'[23] – a phrase with chilling implications. It is also expressly provided that no court of law may pronounce upon the validity of a detention under section 6, nor order the release of a detainee.[24] Further, no person may have access to a detainee,[25] that is, he is held incommunicado. He may not see or even communicate by letter with a lawyer, a private doctor, or a member of his family. Habeas corpus is not permitted.[26] The Act does not authorise physical ill-treatment of detainees,[27] and indeed assault and torture as a means of interrogation have been officially disavowed by the South African government and by senior police officers. The official attitude is that the only sanction available against a recalcitrant detainee is his continued indefinite detention in solitary confinement, without books, letters, newspapers, or any communication with the outside world.[28] In any country, however, if detained persons have no access to lawyers or to the courts, abuses are bound to occur – as they undoubtedly have in South Africa.

Section 6 detention has a profound effect on the conduct of trials under the Terrorism Act. First, the accused himself will probably have been detained in solitary confinement for weeks, months, or sometimes even years before he is brought to trial. Unless he is a person of extraordinary fortitude, he will probably have made a statement to the police, often in the form of a confession, whether false or true. He is unlikely to understand the rules relating to the admissibility in evidence of his statement. In a disquieting recent development, the police have brought some detainees straight from weeks or months of detention to a court, without giving notice to their friends and families. The detainees have then and there been called upon to plead to a complex charge under the Terrorism Act, without the benefit of legal advice or representation. Only after they have pleaded are they able to obtain representation by counsel. Consequently, persons have pleaded guilty to serious charges under this Act without the benefit of legal advice. Perhaps equally important, many of the prosecution witnesses in these

[23] Ibid.
[24] Ibid, s 6(5).
[25] Ibid, s 6(6).
[26] Ibid, s 6(5).
[27] *Nxasana v Minister of Justice* 1976 (3) SA 745 (D), 748 per Didcott J. *Cf Rossouw v Sachs* 1964 (2) SA 551 (A), 561 (decided under s 17 of the General Law Amendment Act 37 of 1963, an earlier detention statute).
[28] See, eg statement by Mr JT Kruger, then Minister of Justice, in the House of Assembly in May 1978, Hansard (1978) vol 15, cols 7118–21.

trials are persons who have been subjected to prolonged detention in solitary confinement under section 6. Often they too are brought straight from detention to court to give evidence. They will usually have made statements implicating the accused. These statements may be true, but even if they are not, the witness knows that if he retracts, the result may well be either his further detention under section 6 or a charge of perjury.

It is therefore understandable that I have referred to the mode of procedure under this statute as a distortion of South Africa's traditional system of procedure, or as the pathology of a legal system. What has been altered under this new system for trying political offences? To list them briefly: the rules restricting arrest without warrant, the right to be brought before a court speedily after an arrest, the right to bail, the right to legal representation immediately upon arrest, in practice the right to silence, the rule that the burden of proof is on the prosecution, the rule against hearsay evidence, the court's discretion in sentencing, and, along with all of these, the right to habeas corpus. That is to say, a good part of what people in both the United States and South Africa have regarded as essential to a fair trial.The South African government would justify these departures on the ground that subversion is a real threat in South Africa, that important information about unlawful activities has been obtained by this system of detention without trial, and that many of those convicted under the Terrorism Act were in fact engaged in planning acts of violence against the state. Much of this is true, and the South African government is no doubt entitled to some credit for choosing to try political offenders before the ordinary courts of the land. The reason for this choice may be a residual respect for the judicial process. Or it may be the belief that imprisonment after conviction by a criminal court is politically the most persuasive way of disposing of the accused, and the least likely to provoke internal or international criticism. Either way, the choice is not a discreditable one.

II. THE PHILOSOPHY UNDERLYING THE TERRORISM ACT

This choice having been made, however, what is the reasoning behind the new, second-class procedure? It is simply that the more serious the crime, the easier it should be to convict the accused. This view has its adherents in all countries. It has often prevailed, especially in the case of political offenders. And it is an understandable view. As Macaulay wrote, in a trial for treason an acquittal must always be considered a defeat of the government.[29] But until recent years, this was not the prevailing philosophy in South Africa any more than it was in the United States of America. For political crime, the traditional view was the opposite one.

I referred earlier to the two-witness rule in treason cases. This has always been an exception in the English law of evidence[30] which, unlike Mosaic[31] law or the canon law,[32] did not require a multiplicity of witnesses to prove the commission of a crime. Why should there be this exception in the case of treason? The seventeenth century in England was a century of revolutions and revolutionary plots. Charles II, restored to the throne in 1660, had good reason to fear for his security. Yet one of the first acts passed by the Restoration Parliament was an act requiring proof by two witnesses of certain forms of treason.[33] And in 1695 the Whigs themselves enacted the Statute of Treasons, which reinforced the two witness rule and provided that persons accused of treason were to be allowed privileges that they had never before enjoyed, such as the right to counsel.[34] This was at a time when the threat of counter-revolution was real and when the only immediate effect of the new law could be to provide the advantages of a fair trial to the government's most intransigent opponents. Perhaps those legislators thought that one day they might again be in opposition. One may nonetheless think that the passage of this law in England in 1695 constituted one of the highest achievements of that Western civilization of which we in South Africa are said to be amongst the heirs and guardians.

Why should anyone think that a person charged with treason required more protection than persons charged with lesser offences? Sir William Blackstone, writing nearly a century after the Statute of Treasons was passed, gave a straightforward

---

[29] Macaulay, *The History of England* (Westminster edn, nd) 313.

[30] The only other exception to the English law of evidence in modern times has been perjury, which has a history of its own.

[31] Deuteronomy, 17:6, 19:15.

[32] According to Professor CS Kenny of Cambridge, under canon law no cardinal could be convicted of unchastity without at least twelve witnesses, and a woman could not be a witness: C Kenny, *Outlines of Criminal Law*, 19th edn (1966), 519.

[33] Statute of Treasons 1661.

[34] Statute of Treasons 1695.

answer: 'the principal reason undoubtedly is to secure the subject from being sacrificed to fictitious conspiracies, which have been the engines of profligate and crafty politicians in all ages'.[35]

The procedure under the South African Terrorism Act represents a complete reversal of the philosophy behind the Statute of Treasons. It embodies a feeling, popular in many places and times, that the more reprehensible an offence is, the easier it ought to be to obtain a conviction, and that enemies of the government should not be entitled to the ordinary protection of law, but should be placed at a special disadvantage if accused of a political offence. I do not believe that today special privileges are necessary, but to subject the accused to special disabilities and disadvantages is in a measure to condemn him before he has been tried. The removal of the presumption of innocence is very close to the assumption of guilt. One is reminded of the views of that otherwise humane and enlightened French jurist of the sixteenth century, Jean Bodin, on the crime of witchcraft. He said that persons accused of witchcraft ought to be convicted without further proof unless they proved their innocence. For, he said, 'to adhere, in a trial for witchcraft, to ordinary rules of procedure, would result in defeating the law of both God and man'.[36]

Have the extraordinary rules worked in South Africa? From the point of view of the government, the answer is yes. Information has been extracted from detainees that would probably not have been obtained under the ordinary rules, and persons have been convicted who might have gone free under ordinary procedures. Whether this is worth the price paid is a question of political and moral judgment. One's answer will no doubt depend on the importance one attaches to meeting the criteria for what constitutes a highly civilised nation, as proposed by Justice Roberts. A South African judge, referring to section 6 of the Terrorism Act, said:[37]

> In providing for the detention for indefinite periods of those who have not been convicted of crimes, for their isolation from legal advice and from their families, and for their interrogation at the risk of self-incrimination, the Legislature has pursued its object by the enactment of measures which are undoubtedly foreign to the ordinary principles of our law. Whether the end justifies the drastic means that have been sanctioned because they are necessary in troubled times for the

---

[35] W Blackstone, *Commentaries on the Laws of England*, vol 4, 358.
[36] J Bodin, *Demonomanie*, vol 4, ch 4 (1598) quoted in Kenny, n 32 above, 517–18.
[37] *Nxasana v Minister of Justice* 1976 (3) SA 745 (D), 747 per Didcott J.

security of the State, as they are apparently thought by Parliament to be, is a controversial question . . .

Later in the same judgment he said that effect must be given 'to stringent enactments which are positively shown by Parliament's choice of plain words to have been meant, however offensive to conventional legal standards they may be'.[38] He described this conclusion as axiomatic in South African law. On this point he is undoubtedly correct.

III. THE ATTITUDE OF JUDGES AND LAWYERS

This brings me to the last part of this lecture, the approach of the judges and lawyers to legislation of this type. South Africa has, as I have said, no bill of rights. Our political system is one of complete parliamentary sovereignty. No court can declare any of the provisions that I have described unconstitutional. Years ago a South African judge of appeal said that it was the duty of the courts to act as buttresses between the executive and the subject.[39] But how are they to do so in the light of their duty to give effect to parliamentary enactments however draconian and however 'offensive to conventional legal standards'? The answer ordinarily given is that their sole power is the power to interpret those enactments. In the judgment previously quoted, the judge put this in clear language:[40]

> Our Courts are constitutionally powerless to legislate or to veto legislation. They can only interpret it, and then implement it in accordance with their interpretation of it. When there is a real doubt about the meaning of a statute, their tradition is to construe it so that it provides for the least amount of interference with the liberty of the individual that is compatible with the language used. The tradition has been observed for so long, and has permeated so many fields of our law, that it is unnecessary to cite authority for its acceptance.

So this too is axiomatic.

No doubt the question will be asked: how have the South African courts performed this function of strict interpretation *in favorem liberatatis* in the field of the security and procedural legislation with which I have been dealing? In my – I hope sufficiently –

[38] Ibid, 748.
[39] *R v Pretoria Timber Co (Pty) Ltd* 1950 (3) SA 163 (A), 182.
[40] *Nxasana v Minister of Justice* 1976 (3) SA 745 (D), 747.

respectful opinion, their performance has been mixed. If I were to mark them by the Oxford method, I would give them a beta, query beta minus. On the positive side, there has been some attempt to give a restrictive interpretation to those provisions of the Terrorism Act that place the burden of proof on the accused and to ensure that the procedural advantages are not improperly extended. This is at least true of the Appellate Division of the Supreme Court, which has set aside on appeal several verdicts given by trial judges for want of sufficiently convincing evidence of guilt. In upholding these appeals, it has even reversed the trial judge's findings on the credibility of witnesses.[41] Further, although section 6(5) of the Terrorism Act states that no court shall pronounce on the validity of any action taken under section 6 or order the release of any detainee, this section does not preclude the court from enquiring into the lawfulness of treatment that a detainee receives in detention.[42] The court can therefore on suitable evidence enjoin the police from using unlawful methods of interrogation.

On the negative side, however, the courts have shown a marked reluctance to permit evidence of ill-treatment to be given by the person most concerned, namely the detainee himself. In 1964 a case came to the courts under another 'security' statute which, like section 6 of the Terrorism Act, provided for detention without access to lawyer or friend for the purposes of interrogation.[43] The wife of a detainee had received a smuggled note from him saying that relays of policemen had interrogated him for twenty-eight hours on end without allowing him to rest or even to sit down. When he fell to the floor out of exhaustion, the police threw cold water over him and dragged him to his feet. The wife applied urgently for an injunction restraining the police from continuing this method of interrogation. The police made affidavits denying the allegations, and the wife's counsel asked the court to order that the husband be brought to court to give evidence himself. This was refused by the judge, and his refusal was upheld by a majority in the Appellate Division.[44] The ground of refusal was

---

[41] See, eg *S v Mdingi* 1979 (1) SA 309 (A), 317; *S v Essack* 1974 (1) SA 1 (A), 16–17, 20–21; *S v Ffrench-Beytagh* 1972 (3) SA 430 (A), 446. See also *S v Mushimba* 1977 (2) SA 829 (A), in which the Appellate Division set aside a conviction under the Terrorism Act on the ground that the security police had unlawfully obtained material from the defence files through an agent in the defence attorney's office.

[42] *Nxasana v Minister of Justice* 1976 (3) SA 745 (D), 743.

[43] General Law Amendment Act 37 of 1963, s 17.

[44] *Schermbrucker v Klindt* 1965 (4) SA 606 (A), affirming 1965 (1) SA 353 (T).

that to have the detainee brought to court would interfere with the object of the statute – continuous detention, in isolation, for the purposes of interrogation. Whether this was an inevitable conclusion, having due regard for the terms of the statute, may be judged in the light of the fact that two judges of appeal, including the present Chief Justice,[45] wrote powerful dissents.

In a later case the fathers of some young men detained under section 6 of the Terrorism Act applied to the Transvaal court for an injunction to restrain the police from assaulting the detainees during their interrogation. Because of the earlier case, the applicants asked not that the detainees be brought to court but merely that affidavits be taken from them by a government official. The court held that the Act prevented any such affidavit being placed before it.[46] In other cases also the requirements of the interrogators would seem to have been placed above those of the detaince. It is enough to mention just one more – a much-criticised opinion of the full Bench of the Eastern Cape High Court in which that court held that the threat of further detention did not make the detainee's confession anything but freely or voluntarily made, and thus admissible against him.[47]

These cases give some indication of the judicial approach to the Terrorism Act and to similar statutes. They show judges about their ordinary business of interpreting statutes, evaluating evidence, and reaching varying conclusions. But, it may be asked, what do they feel about these forms of procedure, and especially about indefinite pretrial detention incommunicado, which have so distorted the traditional legal standards they were trained to follow? One may of course ask the same question about the many statutes embodying racial discrimination which the judges are compelled to apply, whatever the hardship those statutes cause. The answer is that on the whole the judges do not say. No doubt some of them regard this legislation as justifiable and proper. Others do not and occasionally hint as much. Some judges who have to enforce these laws emphasise that they are bound by Parliament's law and have no option but to apply it. For example, in a recent case a judge upheld the conviction of an Indian man

---

[45] Mr Justice Frans L Rumpff.

[46] *Cooper v Minister of Police* 1977 (2) SA 209 (T). This case was decided in 1974, but not reported until 1977. More recently, a Natal judge has refused to follow this decision: *Nxasana v Minister of Justice* 1976 (3) SA 745 (D), 753–55, per Didcott J.

[47] *S v Hlekani* 1964 (4) SA 429 (E), decided under the General Law Amendment Act 37 of 1963, s 17. The correctness of this decision was left open in *S v Alexander* 1965 (2) SA 796 (A), 814.

for unlawfully renting an apartment in a 'white' area, and ordered his ejectment although the evidence showed that no habitable accommodation was available to him and his family in the 'Indian' area of his city. In giving judgment, the judge said:[48]

> An Act of Parliament creates law but not necessarily equity. As a judge in a court of law I am obliged to give effect to the provisions of an Act of Parliament. Speaking for myself, and if I were sitting as a court of equity, I would have come to the assistance of the appellant. Unfortunately, and on an intellectually honest approach, I am compelled to conclude that the appeal must fail.

This passage echoes the statement of the great dissenter in *Dred Scott v Sanford*,[49] Justice McLean. A lifelong opponent of slavery, Justice McLean excused or explained his enforcement of the fugitive slave laws as follows: 'With the abstract principles of slavery, courts called to administer this law have nothing to do.'[50] '[T]he hardship and injustice supposed arises out of the institution of slavery, over which we have no control. Under such circumstances, we cannot be held answerable.'[51]

This reasoning did not go unscathed in the United States, nor has it, entirely, in South Africa. In 1971 a Durban law professor asked, in a public address, whether the time had not come for judges to stand up in defence of the rule of law and to say something about an institution, the Terrorism Act, 'which they must surely know to be an abdication [*sic*] of decency and justice'.[52] In particular, he suggested, the judiciary could make the Act less useful, to the authorities 'by denying, on account of the built-in intimidatory effect of unsupervised solitary confinement practically all creditworthiness to evidence procured under those detention provisions'.[53] At that time, as the professor knew, a trial under the Terrorism Act was in progress in which allegations had been made that the police had intimidated state witnesses while in detention. The melancholy result, for the professor, was that he was prosecuted on a charge of attempting to obstruct justice. The prosecution's theory was that he was exhorting the judge to disregard admissible evidence and thus to act improperly. On this

---

[48] *S v Adams* (TPD, unreported, September 1979).
[49] 60 US 393 (1857), McLean J dissenting.
[50] *Miller v McQuerry*, 17 F Cas 335, 339 (1853).
[51] Ibid, 340.
[52] Address by Professor Barend van Niekerk, quoted in *S v van Niekerk* 1972 (3) SA 711 (A), 716.
[53] *S v van Niekerk* 1972 (3) SA 711 (A), 716–17.

theory, the professor was prosecuted and convicted. The judge who tried his case said that 'in a society such as ours' it was not for judges to take sides in public controversies. Nevertheless, he said, this did not mean that a judge must acquiesce in legislation of a really monstrous kind; his way out would then be to resign.[54]

I know of no South African judge who has in fact found any law so monstrous as to compel him to resign.[55] I do not say this as a criticism of individual judges, least of all as a criticism of those whose minds are troubled by the laws that they have to apply. After all, Justices Story and McLean did not feel called upon to resign from the Bench rather than enforce the fugitive slave laws.[56] And one is grateful for those judges who have done what they can to mitigate the harshness of the South African system. The only generalisation in which I shall indulge is that if one participates in a system that distorts justice, truisms about the limited functions of a judge will not necessarily save one's soul.

What of the Bar? What do they do when they get into court, under the heavily loaded rules of the Terrorism Act? The answer is: the best they can. Lawyers tend to play by the rules of the game; when the rules change, they try to win under the new rules. Indeed, one forgets occasionally that it is a different game. The court looks the same, witnesses are examined and cross-examined, lawyers address the court and cite authority. But the realities break through. A fifteen-year-old boy is called as a state witness. It turns out that he has been in solitary detention for three months before being brought to court. Or the accused are acquitted and discharged by the court, but when they leave the courtroom they are immediately re-arrested and detained. What has the exercise in court been worth?

In this regard, South African lawyers, including those who defend in political cases, have, like judges, had to face a fundamental attack on the part they play in the South African system. Mr Joel Carlson, a South African attorney, who over many years had given service to his clients in political trials in South Africa, eventually went into exile. He considered that his work as a

[54] *S v van Niekerk* (DCLD, unreported 13 Dec 1971) per Fannin J.

[55] Sir Robert Tredgold, then Chief Justice of the Federation of Rhodesia and Nyasaland, resigned in 1980 in protest against the Southern Rhodesian Law and Order Maintenance Act 53 of 1960. He felt that it 'would compel the Courts to become party to widespread injustice'. R Tredgold, *The Rhodesia That Was My Life* (1968) 232. Whether the provisions or that Act go beyond those of the corresponding South African statutes is a good point.

[56] See R Cover, *Justice Accused* (1975) esp chs 7 and 13.

defence lawyer 'was assisting the regime to present an overall image, at home and overseas, of judicial integrity and a fair legal system'.[57] Others have echoed this view. The question raised, of course, does not apply only to lawyers. What is anyone's duty in a society that he believes to be unjust and that he does not believe can be changed by any effort of his? In *The First Circle*, Solzhenitsyn has a character say:

> What is the most precious thing in the world? It seems to be the consciousness of not participating in injustice. Injustice is stronger than you are, it always was and it always will be; but let it not be committed through you.[58]

PW Botha's South Africa is not by any means Stalin's Russia, but even so, this austere imperative is not easy to live by. For judges it may be impossible, and, if Mr Carlson is right, perhaps for practising lawyers too. Possibly our participation in the distorted legal process I have described does give it some respectability. I hope this is not so, but if so, what is the alternative? Must one refuse to take any part in these trials? A mere practising advocate cannot very satisfactorily explore the ethical and social ramifications of this question, much less offer a generally satisfactory solution. He must fall back on the traditional ethics of his profession, not to answer the question but to evade it.

The answer is one that more appropriately comes from his clients. For the most part, the attitude of defendants in South African political trials has been that they wish to be defended – to be acquitted if possible, and, if not, at least to get the minimum sentence. There have been cases, however, in which the defendants have refused to recognise the jurisdiction of the court. These, so far, have been exceptional. This may change. A recent and disquieting tendency in South African political trials has been to exclude the public (although not the press) from the court and to forbid the press from publishing the names of state witnesses. The ground given for these rulings is the fear that those witnesses will be harmed or even killed by the political associates of the accused. In the most recent major political trials, in Pietermaritzburg last September, when the judge ordered the public to be excluded from the court, all the defendants dismissed their counsel and refused to take any further part in the proceedings. This attitude may become more common. But as long as defendants want the

---

[57] J Carlson, *No Neutral Ground* (1973), 362.
[58] A Solzhenitsyn, *The First Circle* (Fontana, 1970) ch 55, 418.

services of an advocate, he is not to refuse them. And if it be said that by so doing he is bolstering up an unjust system, that is one more burden of an onerous profession.

By way of summing up, I limit myself to two propositions. One is obvious – in the absence of an entrenched bill of rights, the judiciary is a poor bulwark against a determined and immoderate government. The other is not so obvious, at least in South Africa. It is that legislation such as I have described does more than restrict judges' legal power to protect the liberties of the subject: it increasingly undermines their will to do so, even when it may still be possible. Too soon they accept a position of subordination and unprotesting powerlessness. And this has a reciprocal effect. Judge Learned Hand once said '[a] society whose judges have taught it to expect complaisance will exact complaisance'.[59]

That is the great loss. One day there will be change in South Africa. Those who then come to rule may have seen the process of law in their country not as protection against power but as no more than its convenient instrument, to be manipulated at will. It would then not be surprising if they failed to appreciate the value of an independent judiciary and of due process of law. If so, then it may be said of those who now govern that they destroyed better than they knew.

Is there any hope of restoring what has been lost? It would not be realistic to say so. But realism, however sombre, is not to be confused with silence or acquiescence. 'It is not necessary to hope in order to work, and it is not necessary to succeed in order to hope in order to work, and it is not necessary to succeed in order to persevere.'[60]

~

---

[59] L Hand, 'The Contribution of an Independent Judiciary to Civilization', in *The Spirit of Liberty*, 3rd edn (1960) 163.
[60] Attributed to William of Orange (1533–1584).

2

*The South African Bar: A Moral Dilemma?**

~

NOTWITHSTANDING THE SOMEWHAT portentous
title which has been given to this talk, I fear that it is
likely to be anecdotal rather than philosophical. Nor is
it intended to be an exercise in comparative law – although if
anyone wishes to draw analogies or even draw a moral from it
they are welcome to do so.

Comparisons indeed are not difficult. In South Africa the legal
profession and the Bench in many ways resemble their English
counterparts. In the first place, there is a divided profession –
there are advocates (barristers) who have sole rights of audience
in the Supreme Court and who take briefs only from attorneys
(solicitors). Up to the time South Africa became a republic in
1961, Leading Counsel had the title of QC – Queen's Counsel.
Since then, the title has been SC – Senior Counsel. The Judges of
the South African Supreme Court (equivalent to the High Court
in England) are by law required to be qualified advocates and by
convention (only occasionally broken) are chosen from among practising Senior Counsel. And, although the common law of South
Africa is the Roman-Dutch law, the law of evidence and of civil
and criminal procedure is in general English law – perhaps the
greatest and most lasting legacy of the English presence in South
Africa. One major difference is that, for various reasons, juries
were abolished long ago. In a criminal as in a civil case, the judge
is the trier of fact. This is not without advantages when one is
trying to reverse a finding of fact on appeal. Save for the absence
of the jury (and of wigs), you would find the look of a South

---

* This was an informal talk given at the Middle Temple in January 1986.

African court and its procedure quite familiar. But, although it seems to be much the same, in one fundamental respect it is very different indeed. And that, I suppose, is what this talk is about. The fundamental difference, of course, is that the practice of law and the whole legal and judicial system is set in the matrix of the laws of apartheid.

You will have heard that in recent times there have been reforms in South Africa. That is not untrue. But the basic laws of apartheid remain and are still vigorously enforced. I shall not attempt to summarise the laws of apartheid. I shall content myself with saying that it is a system which not merely permits racial discrimination but in many of the most important aspects of life requires it. Thus it requires residential segregation and school segregation; it lays down, subject to some limited exceptions, that for blacks to enter and work in an urban area is not a right, but a privilege. Whole black communities may be removed from one area to another without their consent. And there is that other peculiar institution – indefinite detention for interrogation without warrant or charge and without the right to see a lawyer or anyone else. Again, while in many respects there is freedom of speech and a free press – visitors to South Africa are often surprised by this – there is nonetheless a complex web of restrictions on what a newspaper may report. And many other laws exist which are doubtless well known to you.

Why do these laws create anything which could be called a dilemma for the Bench and Bar? In every country, including this one, there are laws of which members of the Bar and Bench may disapprove and which they wish to see changed. The distinction, I believe, is that the laws which I have described are regarded by many lawyers not merely as undesirable or unfair, but as so immoral and unjust as to be totally abhorrent. Apartheid brings into conflict with the law people who in the ordinary way would not be classed as revolutionaries, let alone criminals. I can illustrate this from my own professional experience. In my time at the South African Bar I have defended in almost every type of criminal case, from drunken driving through fraud to murder. But I have also had among my clients – and I am not here speaking of libel actions or suchlike, but of criminal cases properly so called where the accused stands in the dock – at least seven of the editors of leading and respectable South African newspapers, two law professors, a leading QC, and an Anglican dean.

The question is, under such a system how far should a lawyer go in upholding these laws?

I do not wish to give a wrong impression. The South African Bar is not a collection of forensic Prufrocks, picking at their consciences. Most of the time a South African advocate appears in ordinary cases about insolvency or burglary or insurance or patents. But there are enough of the other type of cases to force one at times to think a little more deeply about what one is doing as an advocate. Here I should say that another heritage which we have from the Bar of England is the cab-rank rule. I am absolutely certain that in South Africa, where there have been so many trials of an overtly political nature, the rule is essential: it ensures that accused persons in such cases do not merely have a defence but are properly and fearlessly defended. It is not that in the absence of such a rule the accused would not get a defence at all. It is rather that in some types of case – particularly in treason trials, of which there are many in South Africa – defending counsel is sustained and strengthened by the understanding of his professional colleagues – among whom for these purposes I include the judges – that what he is doing for his client, however much it may hurt or offend persons in authority, is no more than his duty. The rule also ensures that the independence of the advocate is generally recognised even by the public at large – the advocate is not necessarily associated with the views of his client. This may seem pusillanimous. Why should we care what anyone thinks of us? If we all had the courage of an Erskine or a Clarence Darrow, we should not require that sort of protection. But I assure you that for ordinary mortals the support of this professional tradition can be very comforting indeed.

But let me get back to the dilemma. Where the doubts creep in is when one considers the cab-rank on the other side of the street. Ordinarily the cab-rank rule requires one to take cases for the state as well as for the individual. In the many ordinary cases in which government is involved there is no difficulty about this, even in South Africa. But does the cab-rank rule require an advocate to take a brief designed to enforce apartheid laws? What if one is offered a brief to appear for a public authority in proceedings to eject a respectable Indian family from their home on the sole ground that their home is in an area in which it has been declared that only whites may live? Or consider proceedings under the statute which is the cornerstone of the apartheid system – the Population Registration Act 1950. Since 1950 every inhabitant of South Africa has been classified in a central registry according to his or her racial group – for example, as white or black or coloured (ie of mixed race) or Indian. This classification determines whether one may vote, where one can live, to what school one may send one's children, and (until last year) it determined whom one might marry or cohabit with. Under this Act there is a tribunal which has jurisdiction to alter classifications. Frequently the authorities seek to reclassify a person from white to coloured or coloured to black, ie a reclassification which would in each case increase the disabilities of the person concerned. Such a reclassification can be calamitous in the South African context. It may mean moving home, moving schools, severing associations and possibly losing a job. In short, it means expulsion from one's community. The procedure before this tribunal often includes a humiliating physical examination designed to establish so-called racial characteristics. The government has sometimes briefed counsel to obtain such a reclassification from the tribunal. Is counsel obliged to take such a case? I can only say that I hope not. I, happily, have never been asked to take such a brief. If refusal of it were a breach of Bar rules, I can only hope that, if I had ever been asked to take such a brief, I would have had the firmness to break the rules. And how must one regard a colleague who does take such a case when he knows that his efforts are directed at the probable ruin of people who have committed no crime other than to be born the wrong colour? Is the cab-rank rule sufficient to pacify his conscience?

Some lawyers, particularly black lawyers, have themselves come into conflict with the law. One such case with which I was concerned arose out of a treason trial in Natal. The prosecution called as a witness a young black attorney. He and the accused (also a young black man) were close friends. The attorney was not alleged by the prosecution to be an accomplice; he was called only to give evidence that the accused had been in possession of a particular motor car at a particular time. He was unwilling to give any evidence at all. He told the court that he believed that, however serious the crime the accused had committed, it was a crime of conscience. In his own community, as he explained to the judge, the accused was not regarded as a criminal. And in any event he could not bring himself to give evidence against his close friend. He knew that to refuse to give evidence would result in a prison sentence for himself and in the event he was sentenced to three years' imprisonment for contempt of court. That was what the law then provided for.

The next development was that the Natal Law Society, acting on a majority vote of its executive committee, moved in the Natal Supreme Court to strike him off the role of attorneys. The test in a striking-off application, it was accepted, was whether the practitioner had shown himself to be unworthy to remain a member of an honourable profession. I was briefed for the attorney. My argument in his defence was that, although his refusal to give evidence was plainly unlawful, his behaviour had been frank and honest, and dictated by his conscience and not by disrespect for the court: his conduct did not suggest that he was a person who would be likely to mislead the court, or to cheat or betray a client. The argument of the Law Society was that it was the duty of an attorney to further the law and not to obstruct it: his failure to do so, particularly in a treason trial, was inconsistent with his position as an attorney and an officer of the court. This was a powerful argument. The Law Society's application was heard, as was usual, by a bench of two judges; they disagreed. It was re-argued before a different bench of three judges. The Law Society's application was dismissed by 2 to 1. It was not an easy question. I imagine that in a similar case English judges might also be divided.

What of the Bench? I am speaking now of the Supreme Court Bench, not the magistracy. The South African Supreme Court Bench has a high reputation. This derives in large measure from the judgments of the Appellate Division in cases involving civil liberties in the 1950s, when the court was presided over by Mr Justice Centlivres. Last autumn, in his Francis Mann lecture, Sir Robert Megarry said – and I think proved – that there were no longer political appointments to the Bench in England. There have been far too many in South Africa. There have been cases of obvious political favour and some where the appointee had no discernible qualifications other than his political affiliation. Fortunately such appointments do not represent a majority of the Bench. There are members of the South African Bench who could fittingly sit on any court in the world. But the studied and obvious departure from merit as the sole criterion for appointment to the Bench has undoubtedly lowered its status. This factor, together with the nature of some of the laws which a judge must enforce, has deterred some highly qualified candidates from accepting appointments to the Bench. For my part, I am grateful that many good men have accepted appointments, not least those who are plainly disturbed by the nature of some of the laws which they have to enforce. Nonetheless, the moral duty of the Bench has become a subject of debate in South Africa, at least in the law journals. Some academic and other critics have suggested that any South African judge who truly believes in justice and the rule of law is in conscience bound to resign. Apart from being impractical, this seems to me to be a childishly simplistic prescription. Nonetheless, there is no doubt that some South African judges see in their situation a moral problem which is not necessarily overcome by saying that they are not responsible for the laws of the land.

Similar advice has been given to members of the South African Bar by critics both in and outside the country. It has been pointed out with substance that the corrupting influence of apartheid permeates the judicial system as it does every other institution. The judicial system, they say, is loaded against blacks not least in the criminal courts and most obviously in the imposition and carrying out of capital punishment. This is a touchy subject in South Africa, but I believe that there is much truth in this criticism. However, the critics argue from this that the Bar, by carrying out its functions in the courts of South Africa, gives a veneer of spurious respectability to an unjust system. This may be so, but if the apparent corollary is that the advocate, like the judge, must simply resign from this system, I find it hard to accept. I consider that there are two practical questions which a lawyer might ask himself. First, is there a reasonable chance of obtaining redress in the courts for the individual in conflict with the government? In particular, in a political prosecution is there a reasonable chance of obtaining an acquittal? Or is the legal process a mere charade? The answer in South Africa is that it is not hopeless. An expert on Soviet law once told me that in the Soviet Union the rate of convictions in all courts was 98%. He was entirely unable to account for the 2% of acquittals. That is not so in South Africa. Take trials for treason. Loaded as the dice may be, there have been many acquittals in treason trials in South Africa, notably in Pietermaritzburg last month, when a major treason prosecution upon which the government had set great store had to be withdrawn by the Attorney-General following the judge's rulings on the indictment and on the inadmissibility of evidence on which the prosecution was heavily relying. Even under the current emergency regulations judges have found grounds for granting habeas corpus, and have in a number of cases granted injunctions against the police.

The second question which a lawyer might ask is whether those who are most closely affected by the apartheid laws and the security laws wish to be represented by counsel. The answer is that they do. I know of only one case, a trial for terrorism, where the accused for various reasons refused to recognise the jurisdiction of the court. They dismissed their counsel and refused to take any further part in the proceedings other than to disrupt them wherever possible. The judge handled a difficult trial extremely well, save that at the end of it he sentenced to death one of the accused whom he held to be the ringleader in the conspiracy. In fact, on the record he was by no means the ringleader of the conspiracy: he was merely the ringleader of the disruption. At that stage, the man who was sentenced to death thought that he had better go on appeal and thought that he had better have counsel to represent him. So it was. The Court of Appeal in fact set aside the death sentence, presumably considering that contempt of court was not a capital offence. If counsel and court in that appeal lent respectability to the system, so be it. The alternative for the appellant would have been somewhat stark.

I am conscious that I have not answered the question set me, but I hope that I have at least explained why it arises.

3

*Civil Rights in Southern Africa: The Prospect for the Future**

~

T
HE FUTURE OF Southern Africa is a dark and difficult subject. I have taken as the title for this lecture one
relatively narrow aspect of it. What I intend to discuss
is the prospect for the recognition and legal protection of civil
rights, but in doing so I can hardly avoid some consideration
of the political future of Southern Africa. One seldom does that
without acquiring strong political opinions or prejudices. These
will doubtless emerge. But I hope that they will be modified by
a lawyer's objectivity and a present distance of 6,000 miles. I
shall speak principally of the Republic of South Africa, where I
have lived for most of my life, but I shall refer to other countries,
especially Zimbabwe, where they provide comparisons or indicate
what possibly might lie ahead.

The term 'civil rights' is itself full of problems. Are the right
to work and to freedom from poverty civil rights which should be
legally protected? In the United States, Professor Charles Black
has forcefully argued that there is a constitutionally protected
right to a reasonable livelihood.[1] I shall not enter into those
realms. First things first, and especially in Southern Africa, what
I have in mind are rights which most of us would, without precise
definition, accept as fundamental rights. These rights would
include: the right not to be imprisoned, save after conviction on

---

* The annual John Foster lecture, named after an eminent Queen's Counsel, was
instituted and has been continued by his former colleagues and friends. This was the
first of the series, and was delivered in London on 4 November 1986.

[1] See C Black, 'Further Reflections on the Constitutional justice of Livelihood' (1986)
86 *Columbia Law Review* 1103.

29

a defined charge and a fair trial; the right not to be inhumanly treated; the right not to be legally discriminated against on the grounds of colour or race; the right of free movement; the right to private property; the right to freedom of speech; and the right to some form of representation in the government of one's country. For a large part of the population of the Republic of South Africa some of these rights do not exist at all, while others exist only in attenuated form. I take it as self-evident that respect for these rights, in the largest measure compatible with life in an organised society, is desirable. I know, of course, that this proposition is not really self-evident. But it is my starting point, and I shall assume that it is yours.

The protection of these rights by law does not necessarily depend upon constitutional entrenchment. The rights which I have mentioned have in some measure been protected in this country by the common law as applied by the courts. This is true of South Africa too. But in South Africa, as in the United Kingdom, the arguments for a constitutional bill of rights are gathering force. In South Africa the arguments have perhaps a sharper edge. For example, the question of whether whipping should be prohibited as a cruel and inhumane practice arises from circumstances more acute than the imposition of correction on a schoolboy by a school teacher.

It may seem surprising that the first John Foster lecture should deal with an area of the world which, in the field of civil rights, may be classed as underdeveloped. It is not for me to ask why I was invited to give this lecture, but there are, objectively, good reasons why South Africa is so often in the forefront of discussions on civil rights. It is not merely because of the historical connections between this country and South Africa, nor even this country's responsibility for having launched the Union of South Africa in 1910. The interest in South Africa is international, and cuts across all conventional divisions of the east and west or north and south. 'Why should this be?' is the question so often and so plaintively asked in South Africa. I shall try to give a brief answer.

Human rights have become a major subject of international concern only since the end of the Second World War. This can be verified by a glance at the earlier editions of any of the standard textbooks on international law. Even the 1953 edition of Briggs' *Cases and Materials on International Law* has scarcely a mention of human rights, and then only in relation to the treatment of aliens. The change no doubt arose from the revulsion against the horrors perpetrated by the Nazis in Europe. It derived also, I believe, from the wartime experiences of colonial territories.

The Charter of the United Nations states that the observance of fundamental rights and freedoms is one of the objects of the organisation. In 1948 the members of the United Nations were called upon to express their commitment to human rights by approving the Universal Declaration of Human Rights. This Declaration was followed by the European Convention on Human Rights and since then by many other international instruments. These declarations cover a wide range of rights. But in the post-war world the one human right which has internationally become the dominating right is the right to freedom from racial discrimination and, in particular, from discrimination on the grounds of colour. It was not always so.

After the Great War the Covenant of the League of Nations required religious equality to be observed in the Mandated Territories. Japan, an ally in good standing at that time, proposed a clause providing also for racial equality. The Japanese proposal was contemptuously brushed aside. Article 55 of the United Nations Charter and Article 2 of the Universal Declaration embody what was refused in 1919.

South Africa has stood alone in refusing to accept racial equality as a fundamental right. I do not for a moment mean that racial discrimination is practised only in South Africa. For all I know, there may be worse forms of it elsewhere. But South Africa is peculiar in that discrimination on the ground of race in both private and public life has been not only legally permissible but legislatively imposed. Notwithstanding recent reforms, that is so even today. Only a few weeks ago President Botha repeated that residential segregation, school segregation, and the exclusion of blacks from the central political process were not negotiable. And that is the core of apartheid.

South Africa was a founding member of the United Nations – General Smuts was one of the draftsmen of the Charter. But the Nationalist government which came into power in 1948 refused to adhere to the Universal Declaration – joined by Saudi Arabia and the Soviet Union and its satellites. One may see in this refusal a refreshing absence of hypocrisy, especially when one recalls some of the countries that did adhere to the Universal Declaration. But, commendable as it may be to abstain from hypocrisy, it did not save South Africa from incurring a special opprobrium, intensified further by the fact that the people discriminated against in South Africa were and still are a voteless majority ruled by a minority of another race and colour.

There is another factor too. The black population of South Africa has not exactly acquiesced in its subservient status. Consequently, in order to maintain the status quo, it has been necessary for the South African government to assume powers of a type regarded as extraordinary in Western countries. These powers include the power to ban political organisations, the power to place individuals under house arrest, and, above all, the power to detain persons for the purpose of interrogation, without judicial warrant, without limit of time, and without the right of access to a lawyer or anyone else. In an exchange of letters with one of her own backbenchers in 1983, Mrs Thatcher summed up the current state of South African affairs by saying that 'South Africa, by its institutionalised separation of the races, and the repressive measures used to enforce this policy, is a unique case and one which arouses particular emotion in the international community'.

There is another aspect of South Africa which is of peculiar interest. It is the paradox of the co-existence with discrimination and repression of a large degree of freedom of speech; of a press which, save in a state of emergency, is comparatively free and critical; and, above all, of an independent Supreme Court to which an individual may resort – not infrequently with success – for protection against state action. This is a paradox because the South African government, despite its complete parliamentary power and its lack of enthusiasm for any of these institutions, chooses to reluctantly tolerate them.

There are historical reasons for this degree of toleration which are too complex to examine here. But it undoubtedly owes much to the desire of the South African government to be seen as part of the Western World. This desire also accounts for that 'double standard' of which the South African government so often complains. Why pick on South Africa in a world which includes (to take a random choice among the lesser powers) Uganda, Chile, and Poland? A trenchant answer was given by Mrs Thatcher: 'Since the South Africans assert that they belong to the Western World, they must be expected to be judged by Western standards.'

Let me at this point say a word about the South African legal system. The following applies not only to the Republic of South Africa, but to Zimbabwe and the other surrounding states of Botswana, Lesotho, and Swaziland. In these countries two great systems of law are found, both of which place a high value on the liberty of the individual. The common law of these countries is the Roman-Dutch law. It is not always understood that equality under the law is one of the fundamental precepts of that system. After the Dutch, the British brought with them to Southern Africa the inestimable benefit of English civil and criminal procedure, including the basic concept of a fair trial. An independent judiciary also came from Britain. As early as 1832 in the Cape Colony, judges were appointed to hold office *quamdiu se bene gesserit* (during good behaviour) and not merely *durante bene placito* (at the King's pleasure).

Under these two systems of law the courts have often been able to protect individuals, both black and white, against the excesses of executive power. The need to do so, I may add, was there long before the present South African government came to power. How did the courts accomplish this in the absence of a bill of rights? They did it much as the courts have done it in England – by scrutinising the exercise of power to ensure that it was within statutory or prerogative authority; by a narrow construction of statutes impairing the liberty of the subject; by a presumption of equality before the law; and by applying the rules of natural justice, in particular, the maxim *audi alteram partem* (hear both sides).

In 1879 there had been an uprising of the Griquas in territory bordering the eastern Cape Colony, which had been annexed by Britain. Two captured Griquas had been brought to Cape Town, ostensibly as prisoners of war. They were held in a military prison without warrant and on no criminal charge. Sir Henry de Villiers, Chief Justice, issued a writ of habeas corpus and on the return day ordered their release. The Crown had argued that the prisoners were dangerous, and the country was in an unsettled state. But Sir Henry de Villiers said:[2]

> The disturbed state of the country ought not in my opinion to influence the Court, for its first and most sacred duty is to administer justice to those who seek it, and not to preserve the peace of the country . . . The Civil Courts have but one duty to perform, and that is to administer the laws of the country without fear, favour or prejudice, independently of the consequences which ensue.

These words have often been quoted in South African courts, and sometimes they have been applied. They have been especially

[2] *In Re Willem Kok and Nathaniel Balie* (1879) 9 Buch 45, 71.

apposite in 1985 and 1986, when, notwithstanding the enormous powers vested in the executive under the statutory states of emergency, there have been numerous cases in which the courts, by applying common-law principles and well-known canons of statutory interpretation, have been able to order the release of detained persons or to set aside emergency regulations as ultra vires.

These are all good examples of the protection of civil rights, notwithstanding the absence of a bill of rights. But that, of course, is not the whole story. The grounds on which executive acts or regulations can be invalidated are limited. In South Africa, as in other countries, there are some judges who are, in Lord Atkin's phrase, 'more executive-minded than the executive', or those for whom 'state security' are the magic words which close all doors.

There is also that other part of the British legacy, namely, the supremacy of Parliament – which is to say the supremacy of the majority party in Parliament. Since 1948 the government has not hesitated to use its parliamentary power to reverse inconvenient decisions of the courts, particularly those decisions which have struck down racially discriminatory measures. For example, in 1953 Parliament passed a statute known as the Reservation of Separate Amenities Act which provided that public premises or public vehicles could be racially segregated, and which expressly stated that inequality of treatment was not a ground for invalidity. Numerous statutes have, as direct reactions to court decisions, expressly excluded the rules of natural justice for purposes of detention, banning orders and other administrative actions.

This is surely enough to demonstrate that, as valuable as the judicial process has been, in the absence of an entrenched bill of rights the judiciary is an inadequate bulwark against a determined and immoderate government.

What difference would a bill of rights have made in South Africa? It would have invalidated the laws permitting indefinite detention without trial and, at least, the grosser measures of discrimination in relation to education, residence, and employment. It would have prevented the forced deprivation of citizenship which followed the creation of the so-called independent homeland states for blacks. And it would surely have prevented the cruellest manifestation of apartheid – the forcible removal of over four million people from their homes to distant and forlorn resettlement areas.

I have said 'surely'. But this assumes, of course, a bill of rights that was not merely on the statute book, but was fully enforced by the courts and obeyed by the government. However, constitutions and bills of rights, like other statutes, are subject to changing modes of interpretation and, in particular, to changing concepts of constitutional purpose. The United States provides sufficient evidence of this reality.

This is far from denying the value of a bill of rights. It is simply a suggestion that one should not expect too much from even an entrenched bill of rights. Certainly, we should avoid the fallacy that freedom is necessarily broader and better protected in a country with a bill of rights than in a country without a bill of rights. The late Hedley Bull pointed out that, while one could discuss human rights both in the moral sense and the legal sense, one should not overlook a third sense, namely, rights in the empirical sense, that is to say, 'rights that we know from experience and observation to be observed and implemented'. I would add, 'or not implemented, as the case may be'. In order to assess the real state of human rights in any particular country, one may get more enlightenment from the annals of Amnesty International than from the high-sounding professions of national constitutions. Theodore Roosevelt once said that there is a lot of law at the end of a nightstick.

I referred earlier to a 'determined and immoderate government'. In a unitary state, as distinct from a state with an elaborate federal structure, a government with enough at stake politically may find the means, whether parliamentary or extra-parliamentary, to overcome the limitations of an entrenched bill of rights. South Africa's close neighbours of Botswana, Lesotho, and Swaziland obtained independence under a standard British post-colonial constitution, with elaborately entrenched provisions for the protection of parliamentary democracy and of individual rights. It stands firm in Botswana, but in both Swaziland and Lesotho the constitutions were simply done away with by the parties in power.

In the 1950s the South African government attempted to remove the entrenched political rights of the coloured people of the Cape without the two-thirds majority of both Houses of Parliament as required by the South Africa Act 1909. This attempt was frustrated by the unanimous judgment of the Appellate Division of the Supreme Court. But both the entrenched provisions of the South Africa Act and the judgment of the Appellate Division were overcome by the expedient of packing not only the upper house (the Senate) but, to make doubly sure, the Appellate Division as well.

So much for the past; what of the future? I have already indicated that I have no particular qualification for predicting the future course of events in South Africa, but that is not ordinarily a deterrent to prophecy. My own predictions, for what they are worth, are cautious enough. First, I do not see revolution around the corner. The South African government is powerful and is determined to maintain its rule by all necessary use of force. It will, I believe, remain in control for many years to come. But, secondly, the ever increasing numbers, and the growing militancy and economic power of the black population, must, in due course, end the present state of affairs. The result will be the existence of a new form of government in which blacks will have a dominant position in accordance with their numbers, whether as a parliamentary majority or otherwise. My own guess is that this is likely to come about by the end of the century.

What are the prospects for the judicial protection of civil rights, both before and after the inevitable changeover? Self-evidently, the answer must depend on what happens in the interim. If there is a protracted civil war, South Africa, as a single political entity, might no longer exist. But I am optimistic enough to believe that, although it is unlikely that change will be entirely non-violent, events in South Africa could well lead to a negotiated settlement. This settlement in turn will lead to a government with a black majority that will take the form of a constitutional government and not a dictatorship. This is a large conclusion. But I must add yet another large statement – the African National Congress is bound to have an important part in that government. This means, as I see it, that there is likely to be a strong, and possibly dominant, socialist element in a future South African government. What is this likely to mean in relation to civil rights?

First, some general observations: the civil rights which I have been discussing are rights that we usually think of in terms of the individuals whose freedom they protect. This, on the whole, is the Western way of thinking about civil rights. It is not the only way. The Third World, especially in Africa, has perhaps concentrated more on the collective rights of peoples. The right of racial equality has been seen not so much as the right of an individual not to be discriminated against on the basis of his race, but rather as the right of a black population to be liberated as a people from colonialism or white rule. Protection from arbitrary executive action may in this context be thought of as attainable merely by throwing off the yoke of an unelected government, rather than by entrenching rights which are enforceable by the individual against an elected government. Further, many black political

thinkers (and not merely Marxists) regard the major problems of
South Africa to be poverty and economic inequality, and believe
these problems could best be redressed not by a bill of rights,
but by means of a redistribution of wealth, possibly in the form
of a nationalisation of major industries. However unpromising
that may seem as a route to economic prosperity, we would be
wrong to ignore this view. It is a powerful element in black political thought in Southern Africa and, in view of the political and
economic history of the region, it is a wholly understandable one.
These considerations help to explain why the current debate on a
bill of rights for South Africa has taken what may seem to be a
curious turn. Over the last fifteen or twenty years an increasing
number of lawyers, and even some judges, have pointed out the
need for a bill of rights in South Africa. This call was taken up
by white opposition parties, other than those to the far right, and
by some black leaders as well. It obtained no response at all from
the government. This was not strange. Most of the government's
cherished racial laws and many of its security laws could obviously not stand against any Western concept of a bill of rights.
In 1978 a leading South African writer on the subject said that
'both an entrenched bill of rights in a federal setting and the less
powerful unentrenched Canadian-type bill of rights must appear
a Utopian dream to South African libertarians at this time'. The
South African public, he said, required education on the advantages of a bill of rights.

Since then the South African public has indeed had an education, although not an academic one. What has educated it has
been the manifest and disastrous failure of the government's
racial legislation and of its security legislation as well. There is
the growing realisation that apartheid has brought only violence
and economic decline and that unbridled police powers not only
do not bring peace but are self-defeating because of the resentment that they create among those subject to them.

So, the call for a bill of rights has broadened. It now comes even
from academics at Afrikaans language universities (hitherto not
in the forefront of the fight for civil rights) and from newspapers
which support the government. Justice Kotze, a recently retired
judge of the Appellate Division, said at a congress in Pretoria this
year that the security legislation of the country had done irrepa-
rable damage. Pardonably exaggerating, he said he believed that
every member of the Bench regretted that there was so strong
a tendency to give executive authorities unbridled discretion to

assail human rights. The answer, he said, lay in the granting of power to the country's highest court to test contraventions of human rights.

Now the government itself has begun to take notice. In April of 1986, the South African Minister of Justice instructed the South African Law Commission to investigate the desirability of the introduction of a bill of rights and the protection of group rights. In September, at the Transvaal Congress of the Nationalist Party, the Minister of Justice said of the introduction of a bill of rights that 'the question was not when, but how'. But he added that human rights are to be dealt with 'not on a universal basis in every respect . . . but also against the socio-economic background that prevails in a particular country' – words which one is ordinarily more accustomed to hearing from thinkers rather more to the left than Mr Coetsee.

His speech, if I may say so, was a sensible one – quite out of place at a Transvaal Congress of the Nationalist Party. But the new popularity of a bill of rights among sections of the white population has unfortunately produced a negative reaction from some black leaders. They interpret this belated concern with a bill of rights as the reaction of a governing group which sees that its time is running out and wants a bill of rights to protect its existing privileges. There is also a feeling that the new interest in a bill of rights places undue emphasis on the protection of property – which in practical terms means the property of whites.

Why, many blacks ask, this sudden enthusiasm for the legal protection of minority rights when, over all the years, the rights of the majority have had little protection from the law? It is not easy to answer this pointed question. But I do not believe that these suspicions are to be equated with a firm rejection of a bill of rights. Although we may be years from real negotiation, most political forces in South Africa (including the African National Congress) speak in terms of an ultimate negotiated settlement albeit, naturally enough, subject to differing conditions precedent. If an entrenched bill of rights would make majority rule more palatable to minorities, it may well have to be accepted by the majority.

This may sound foolishly sanguine. But there is good reason to believe that the African National Congress, notwithstanding the Marxist element in its ranks, does not exclude a bill of rights from its thinking. Possibly the most important single document in black political history in South Africa is a document called the Freedom Charter. It was adopted by the African National Congress in 1955 and is now supported by many black political groups inside the country. It is a document based largely on the Universal Declaration of Human Rights, with the admixture of some basic socialist prescriptions. Among the latter is the statement that 'the mineral wealth beneath the soil, the banks and monopoly industry, shall be transferred to the ownership of the people as a whole'. On the other hand, it also states that 'all people shall have equal rights to trade where they choose, to manufacture and to enter all trades, crafts and professions'. In part, the Freedom Charter expresses what can only be called general aspirations. For example, it demands that 'rent and prices shall be lowered, food plentiful and no one shall go hungry'. Among the provisions which would not be out of place in a constitutional bill of rights are others such as these: every man and woman shall have the right to vote for and stand as candidate for all bodies which make laws; the rights of the people shall be the same regardless of race, colour or sex. No one shall be imprisoned, deported or restricted without fair trial. No one shall be condemned by the order of any government official. The privacy of the house from police raids shall be protected by law.

This is not a sophisticated document, but it is not one to be ignored or despised. The clauses about nationalisation should certainly be taken seriously. A writer who does not speak for the African National Congress but who, I believe, shares a lot of its thinking has recently written in favour of a bill of rights in a democratic (ie in his terms a black-ruled) South African state. But this is what he had to say about the right of property:

> What would be quite inappropriate for a bill of rights [in South Africa] would be a property clause which had the effect of ensuring that 87% of land and 95% of the productive capacity of the country continued to remain in the hands of the white minority. It is one thing to have a guaranteed right to personal property . . . It is quite another to say that one should have a constitutional right to own a gold mine or a farm of 100,000 hectares.

I suspect that a black government of South Africa is likely to think very much on these lines, although it may be influenced by the examples of Zimbabwe and Mozambique, which show that even governments with strong socialist pretensions are compelled to recognise the value of private enterprise and to seek Western aid and investment.

Allowing for all its deficiencies, the growth of support for the

Freedom Charter seems to me a good augury. Of course, it may be that its professions are no more than the easy promises of a party in opposition. It may be that, if that party did come to power, the promises will be forgotten. Or they might be incorporated in a constitution with no machinery to make them effective. Or they may be so hedged with exceptions as to be valueless. Perhaps at this stage it would be useful to look at the experience of Zimbabwe.

Zimbabwe is an example of the conflict between the legal and the empirical in the field of human rights. Section 15 of the Constitution provides that no person shall be subjected to torture or to inhuman or degrading punishment. Yet investigation by, among others, Amnesty International and the American Lawyers' Committee on Human Rights (neither of which organisations is unsympathetic to Zimbabwe) shows that assault upon and torture of detainees by the security police are rife. The fact that the practices described in their reports were inherited from the previous regime is hardly an excuse. In practice, the treatment of political detainees in Zimbabwe, a country with a bill of rights, is not very different from the treatment of political detainees in South Africa, a country with no bill of rights. If I may speak from my professional experience, as well as from the study of other evidence, I would say that for sheer nastiness there is little to choose between the security police of the two countries.

Once again, this raises the question of whether a bill of rights is of any real value in the face of a government of autocratic tendencies which believes, rightly or wrongly, that it is faced with a state of emergency. I should say that the experience of Zimbabwe is yet another lesson that one must not expect too much from a bill of rights. But a reading of the Zimbabwe Law Reports shows that a bill of rights is by no means futile. Let me take one recent example. An attorney who was taking photographs of the scene of an accident involving his client was arrested by members of the Central Intelligence Organisation on suspicion of a breach of the Official Secrets Act. He alleged that he had been assaulted and sued for damages. One of the emergency regulations in Zimbabwe provides for indemnity to any member of the security forces with respect to anything done in good faith for the purposes of the preservation of the security of Zimbabwe. The regulation further empowers the responsible minister to issue a certificate to that effect. Such a certificate is prima facie proof of what it says. In this case, the minister issued just such a certificate. But five justices of the Supreme Court held that, insofar as the regulation left the question of good faith to the subjective determination of the minister, it was unconstitutional and invalid. The certificate was therefore a nullity and the case could proceed on its merits.

The Zimbabwe example contrasted with a similar case which arose in South West Africa, a territory still subject to the laws of the Republic of South Africa. Under the South African Defence Act, any proceeding, whether civil or criminal, instituted against a member of the South African Defence Force is barred if the State President issues a certificate stating that in his opinion the defendant had acted in good faith for the purpose of the prevention of terrorism. Earlier this year, the Attorney General of South West Africa saw fit to indict four members of the South West African Territorial Defence Force on charges of murder. They were alleged to have beaten and kicked their victim to death. The State President, Mr Botha, caused the requisite certificate to be issued, whereupon the criminal prosecution lapsed and the accused persons went free. Unlike the Zimbabwe case, there was no bill of rights against which the certificate could be tested.

The example of Zimbabwe shows us that a bill of rights in such a society is not a dead letter. As long as there is an independent judiciary, it gives a protection which would not otherwise be available. But in the face of a government which shows no commitment to individual liberty in its executive actions, a bill of rights is no guarantee for freedom and justice.

Mr Mugabe has recently announced that the Roman-Dutch criminal law, which he sees as a link with the system of apartheid, is to be supplanted by a socialist system of penal law which will 'replace punishment with rehabilitation and reorientation', not only of criminals but also, in his reported words, 'of other social deviants'. What this will mean in practice and how it is to co-exist with the Declaration of Rights can at present only be a matter for more or less gloomy speculation.

What does this tell us of the prospects for the Republic of South Africa? On the negative side, even if there were a bill of rights, it would be easy enough for a new government, under colour of a real or imagined emergency, simply to apply existing security legislation against its opponents. There are, however, reasons why one may not unrealistically hope for something better.

In the first place, as I have pointed out, the Freedom Charter gives ground for believing that respect for individual rights has some place in the policies of the black opposition. Secondly, the varied racial and social elements in South Africa make it unlikely that in any future constitutional arrangement any one group would be able to take over the monopoly of power which the present South African government enjoys. There is no group in South Africa which has the same dominant position as the Shona-speaking people of Zimbabwe, who make up about three-quarters of that country's population. Whereas Zimbabwe's white population was never above a quarter of a million, which is less than five per cent of the total Zimbabwean population, South Africa's whites are between four and five million, or about fifteen per cent of the total South African population. There are also the considerable coloured and Asian communities. As far as I know, no major black opposition group in South Africa seeks the exclusion of these millions of citizens from the political process. Finally, the tribal divisions among the black population itself, although much exaggerated by the South African government, are not without significance.

Above all, the conflict is one which both sides must ultimately realise cannot be won outright. A military victory against the formidable South African armed forces by black insurgents, or a successful violent revolution in the near future are hardly realistic possibilities. But the government's policy of 'pacification' by a mixture of force and peripheral reforms is just as unlikely to succeed. If the conflict is to continue unresolved, the prospect is thus one of limited but ceaseless violence against the forces of the state and, eventually, the white population. This violence will be reinforced by industrial action and internal boycotts, and will in turn be met by repression of an increasingly violent and unpleasant nature – repression which will have only temporary and local success. This process is likely to entail a lengthening of the present two-year period of conscription for all young white men, many of whom are already unhappy about serving in what they see as the defence of apartheid. In addition, the violence and the unrest would be accompanied by foreign divestment on both economic and political grounds, leading to a decline in the economy and the quality of life for nearly everyone. This prospect, however appalling, is not likely to lead either side to an unconditional surrender. Reason therefore suggests that both sides can be convinced that a negotiated settlement is preferable to an endless conflict. A negotiated settlement would rationally include an agreed upon constitutional structure containing some restraint on absolute parliamentary or executive power.

This optimistic vision may prove to be entirely wrong. It may be argued that the path of rationality is not obvious. Young black militants have introduced two new and fearful terms into South Africa's political vocabulary: the 'necklace' and the bomb in the crowded shopping centre, killing both blacks and whites, are regarded as legitimate revolutionary operations. On the other side, the police resort to tactics of terror – the whip and the shotgun are used against black children without discernible compunction. Some black leaders talk as though victory were around the corner. On the other side, the government, while disavowing the word 'apartheid', clings to its essential doctrines and practices. Those on the right of the government wish to go back to the pure doctrine of apartheid as practised by Dr Verwoerd. One is tempted to say, both of the government and of the right wing, what Gibbon said of another people, that they 'yield a stronger and more ready assent to the traditions of their remote ancestors than to the evidence of their own senses'.

Notwithstanding the foregoing, I believe that South Africa still has time in hand. Although there is already endemic unrest in South Africa, with horrifying violence on both sides, this violence is well short of civil war. Moreover, a significant number of whites, including influential members of the business community and others who were previously at least tacit supporters of the government, are joining with blacks in calling not merely for reform but for the complete dismantling of apartheid, as well as the recognition of and negotiation with the African National Congress. They accept what only a few years ago would have been unthinkable, namely, the extension of political rights to blacks on a one person, one vote basis. If the time left is not to be squandered, I have no doubt that one of the most positive acts which the South African government can be urged to do is to enact at once an effective bill of rights.

By an effective bill of rights I mean a statute which would provide a real restraint on arbitrary executive action; which would preclude indefinite detention without trial; which would prevent forced removals of communities; which would undo bans on political organisations and individuals, so as to allow them to carry on open political activity; and which would dismantle apartheid by making discrimination on the grounds of race or colour actually illegal. Why, it may be asked, should this statute be enacted at this late stage?

I have spoken of the government of Zimbabwe as a government with no real commitment to the protection of individual rights.

The same is still basically true of the South African government, notwithstanding its new openness to a bill of rights. Why should any future South African government have a greater commitment? If individual rights are to be protected, it is the people of the country who must feel that commitment. That commitment may come, I believe, from the experience of a bill of rights in effective operation. In its report on Zimbabwe, the American Lawyers' Committee for Human Rights quotes a Zimbabwean lawyer of long experience who spoke of the operation of law in Southern Rhodesia under the Rhodesian Front government. He said:

> Most blacks grew up thinking the law was the enemy. It never occurred to them to seek redress of their grievances in the courts. It was absurd. They knew it would be fruitless, that the deck was always stacked against them.

The attitude of the black population concerning the law in South Africa is, in my experience, very similar. The instances of judicial protection of individual rights which I have given are not representative of a black person's experience of the law in South Africa. In general, a black person in South Africa is on the receiving end of the law. His ordinary experience of the operation of the innumerable apartheid laws and regulations has taught him that the process of law is merely an instrument of government, there to enforce the dictates of apartheid. If South Africa is to have a government of laws in the future, whatever time is left must be used to ensure that the popular perception of law changes radically – that it is seen as a protector of the individual, especially the black individual.

This brings me back to the factor of international concern. Over the past twenty or twenty-five years, international law and practice have rapidly developed in the direction of recognising the right of the international community to intervene, by any means short of force, to prevent or redress domestic violations of human rights. The existence of the system of apartheid has been central to this departure from the traditional concept of a domestic jurisdiction beyond the reach of international law.

The Declaration on Non-Intervention of the General Assembly of the United Nations in 1965 proclaimed that every state has 'an inalienable right to choose its political, economic, social and cultural systems without interference in any form by another state'. But even this inalienable right is overridden by the superior principle, stated in the same Declaration, that 'all states should contribute to the complete elimination of racial discrimination in all its forms and manifestations'. In the early 1950s, states such as Sweden took the position, in relation to the issue of apartheid, that the United Nations Assembly had no right to request alterations in the domestic laws of a member state. The United Kingdom's view at that time was that the Assembly was not entitled even to discuss the matter.

Now, in 1986, most Western countries consider it legitimate, and indeed a matter of duty, not only to express strong views on apartheid but to assist in bringing it down. Even the governments of the United Kingdom and the United States, which in this sphere prefer restraint to radicalism, have adopted economic measures to that end. In her first address to the United Nations, the President of the Philippines, Mrs Aquino, felt it right to speak of the need for all members to play their part in bringing about change in South Africa. Those governments who do not favour economic sanctions against South Africa are not necessarily opposed to other forms of intervention. As Sir Geoffrey Howe has explained, the dispute is one of method – what is the most effective way of bringing about the ending of apartheid? This attitude assumes that the ending of apartheid will be a good in itself. That is surely right. The wickedness and cruelty of that system are incapable of any defence. But one hopes that the effort of ending apartheid would be rewarded by the emergence of a society in which basic civil rights are respected and enforced. I would say that the best contribution which Western governments could make to this long-term objective is to persuade the South African government, by all appropriate means, to adopt a genuine and effective bill of rights now.

I am conscious that underlying everything that I have said is an acceptance of the Western view of civil and human rights. It has sometimes been said that there is a tendency in Western countries to believe that the human rights problem is essentially the problem of how Western countries are to use their influence to bring the socialist countries and the countries of the Third World into line on human rights. He said, perhaps somewhat scornfully, that the public appeal of human rights as an object of a foreign policy derives in large measure from the belief that the guardianship of human rights in the world is the special vocation of the Western countries. But that seems to me an entirely admirable vocation. It is surely right that Western countries, if their professions are sincere, should use what influence and power they have to persuade other countries of the value of these rights and to induce them to recognise and protect them. In the case of South Africa, the Western nations have a real opportunity to do so. I hope that they will not let it go by default.

POSTSCRIPT

This attempt at political prognostication, while wholly rejected by political commentators, had hits as well as misses. My forecast that there would be a peaceful transfer of power in South Africa and that one of its essential conditions would be agreement on an entrenched constitutional bill of rights proved to be correct. As one of the ministers in Mr Mandela's government acutely observed, the new constitution was a treaty of peace. On the timing of the changeover I was, happily, somewhat off the mark. I had cautiously said 'by the end of the century'. In fact, only four years after my lecture Mr Mandela was released from prison, and four years after that he took office as State President under the new Constitution of South Africa.

4

*Law and Lawyers in a Changing Society**

∽

I T IS AN honour, but also a great sadness, to be delivering the first Ernie Wentzel Memorial Lecture. The sadness is that Ernie Wentzel should have died so early, still in his prime as a man and an advocate. The sorrow caused by his death was not due only to the almost universal popularity in the legal profession which his wit and good humour won him. There was also the sense that we had lost that rare thing, a true leader of our profession. Ernie Wentzel had been Chairman of the Johannesburg Bar Council, and an outstandingly good one. But his leadership was more than formal. He held strong beliefs about the law and about the society in which he practised law. Ernie's beliefs were clear, consistent and uncompromising. A founder member of the Liberal Party, he was and remained a Liberal with a capital L. He detested racism, white or black, and he detested fascism, whether of the right or of the left. Above all, he believed in individual rights and individual choices. Thus it was inevitable that he became a steadfast political opponent of the government and inevitable too that in his profession he should be a forceful defender of the victims of government policies.

The government did not like this; nor did the security police, many of whose members Ernie put through the shredder in the witness box. When, during the Emergency of 1960, the security police first enjoyed the heady power of detention without trial, Ernie was one of those whom they held. He was imprisoned for three months. After the Emergency, the hostility of the government

* This was the first Ernie Wentzel Memorial Lecture, given at the Centre for Applied Legal Studies, University of Witzwatersrand, in 1987.

47

to Ernie continued. His passport was withdrawn and not restored to him for many years.

It may seem superfluous to stress Ernie Wentzel's opposition to detention without trial. Who does not condemn it? But for Ernie it was not merely a matter of who was doing the detaining and who was being detained – he would condemn it whether done by governments of West or East, of left or right, whether by black governments or white governments. Some of his friends on the left found it difficult to accept this uncompromising stance. Ernie, I think, regretted this because he regretted any divisions among opponents of apartheid. He was a practical politician. But on certain basic principles he would not give way.

Ernie Wentzel's experience of the law in South Africa was therefore, like that of most of us here, entirely within the period of nationalist rule. Before venturing to look at the future of the law and lawyers in this country, it would be as well to reflect a little on what has happened to law and the courts in the years since 1948. I propose to do this only in the broadest outline. I shall certainly not attempt a history of the racial laws and the security laws which have been thrust upon us in the era of apartheid. I shall have nothing to say about changes in the common law however important, during this period. I shall confine myself to that part of the law which can compendiously, if not entirely accurately, be called human rights law.

I. THE APPEAL COURT

At the beginning of that period, the Appellate Division was presided over by Watermeyer CJ and, after him, by Centlivres CJ. Justices Schreiner, Greenberg, and van den Heever were members of the court. One would have had to look far to find a court superior in independence and ability. It was this court which held that the attempts of the government to remove the coloured voters from the common roll in the Cape Province were unconstitutional and illegal.[1] They said the same of the government's attempt to circumvent their judgment by creating the so-called High Court of Parliament.[2] This court struck down unauthorised segregation in railway coaches and racial discrimination in the issue of trading licences. In one of the early cases under the

[1] *Harris v Minister of the Interior* 1952(2) SA 428 (A).
[2] *Minister of the Interior v Harris* 1952(4) SA 769 (A).

Suppression of Communism Act, the court invalidated banning orders which had been issued without prior notice.[3] It was this court (to mention just one other great case of the period) which heard the appeal of the late Solly Sachs (a militant left-wing trade unionist) against the attempt of the Minister of the Interior to withdraw his passport.[4] The majority of the court held that under the common law the state, having issued a passport to a citizen, could not take it away without good cause. They ordered Sachs's passport to be restored to him.

It is well known that the South African Supreme Court enjoys a high international reputation. In large measure, this is due to recollections of the Watermeyer and Centlivres court of the early 1950s. And, of course, at that time there were other outstanding judges in the Provincial Divisions who took their cue from the court of ultimate jurisdiction. I do not think that it can be disputed that, within the limits imposed by statute and the common law, the courts provided a real protection to the individual against executive excess.

Nor, I fear, can it be disputed that after the early 1950s there was a falling off, not merely in the willingness of the courts to protect the individual against the executive, but in the status of the courts. There have at all times been some excellent judges at all levels of the Supreme Court; and throughout the period I am speaking of, one can find striking cases where judges of the Supreme Court upheld the rights of the individual against the state. But that there was a general decline, I have no doubt. I shall not attempt to describe the process, but I shall try to give some generalised reasons for that decline.

The first cause was the legislative policy of the government which came into power in 1948. It showed scant regard for the courts. All the judgments of the Appellate Division to which I have referred were effectively reversed by legislation, and in one statute after another government reduced the powers of the courts. In particular, the common law concept of equality before the law was replaced by statutory and compulsory discrimination with which the courts were powerless to interfere, even had they wished to do so.

---

[3] *R v Ngwevela* 1954 (1)SA 123 (A).
[4] *Sachs v Donges* 1950(2) SA 265 (A).

II. CHANGES IN THE COURTS

There was also a significant change in the composition of the Supreme Court. In South Africa, as in other countries, there have always been some political appointments to the Bench, but in the 1950s there was so marked an increase in these appointments – by which I mean appointments explicable only on political grounds – as to make it clear that it was a deliberate policy of the government. Indeed, in this period the Minister of Justice, Mr CR Swart, said openly that it had been his policy to appoint more Afrikaners to the Bench in accordance with their preponderance in the white population. Mr Swart may then be given the credit for the first application of affirmative action in this field in South Africa – long before that expression was coined. Whatever one may think of Mr Swart's motives, the fact is that when judges are selected on any grounds other than ability, judicial standards must fall. In 1955 the government increased the number of Appellate Division judges to eleven, appointing five new judges whose qualifications for promotion could not be detected by the legal profession. The Appellate Division has never quite recovered.

The change in the courts was also attributable to the spirit of the times. Looking back, one can see that by the early 1960s there was a general spirit of submission to authority. The government was all-powerful. Resistance seemed hopeless. Protest became a minority activity among blacks as well as whites. Sharpeville, in March 1960, saw the last major protest against the laws and institutions of apartheid for some sixteen years. Certainly, amongst the majority of the white population there was an assumption that the government and the police knew best. The courts seemed to share this view. Apartheid crept into the courts themselves. In courtrooms throughout the country a wooden bar was placed in the middle of each witness box. The sole object of this was to ensure that any white witness would stand on one side of this bar and any non-white witness on the other side. (Historians looking back on this era will think that this was a manifestation not merely of prejudice, but of actual insanity.) Even worse, in some magistrates' courts, apartheid was applied to black legal practitioners. One such case in 1958 concerned a young black lawyer who came into a magistrates' court to defend his client on a criminal charge. He went to the normal place where attorneys sat. He was directed by the magistrate to sit at a separate table for black practitioners. He refused to do so.

He was there and then convicted of contempt of court. He took an appeal right up to the Appellate Division. By then, Watermeyer CJ and Centlivres CJ had gone. The Chief Justice was Mr Justice LC Steyn. He dismissed the appeal.[5] He held that the magistrate was fully entitled to apply segregation in his court. One will find in his judgment not one word of criticism of the concept of segregation in a courtroom nor any questioning of why a black attorney should be required to sit at a separate table; still less any appreciation of the fact that the black attorney and his black client might feel humiliated and discriminated against. What Steyn CJ said was simply this – that a defence could be conducted as well from one table as from another. Four other Judges of Appeal concurred. But what is most shameful is that this case drew no protest, either from other members of the Bench or from the Bar or the attorneys' profession. We lamely accepted it. There had, incidentally, been a month-long boycott by the Johannesburg Bar of Mr Justice Steyn when he was first appointed to the Transvaal Bench. But this was not because of his degraded view of law and society – that had not yet been revealed – but because he had been appointed not from the Bar, but from the civil service.

In the period which I am talking about, and right through to the 1970s, there are numerous cases in the law reports about race; and the reported cases are of course only a fraction of those that were being heard. These were cases under the Immorality Act, the Race Classification Act and the Group Areas Act, under all of which the race of the person concerned was the major issue. The state zealously prosecuted what we would now call victimless crimes. Judges and, more frequently, magistrates heard evidence about the racial antecedents of the accused persons or litigants before them, their history and their associations. The courts studied and recorded their physical appearance. One would find on the part of the judges and magistrates concerned no discernible distaste for these processes, still less any conception that the laws they were applying were as abhorrent as the laws of slavery.

There is no point in dwelling further on the law as it was applied during those years. I hope I am not over-optimistic when I say that we have passed through and out of that period. The partitions in the witness boxes have gone. I do not believe that any magistrate would today order a black practitioner to sit at

[5] *R v Pitje* 1960(4) SA 709 (A).

a separate table. And if he did, his ruling would not be upheld by the present Chief Justice. The Immorality Act has gone. The Population Registration Act and the Group Areas Act are still very much with us, but cases under them are few and the humiliating processes which I have described seem to have disappeared. And in recent years many of our courts seem to have shown a new willingness to give protection and relief to individuals affected by state action. One can think of cases on the rights of blacks and their families to live in urban areas, even before the repeal of influx control – cases such as the *Komani* case[6] and the *Rikoto* case.[7] And there are the well-known cases where the courts have placed an onus on the state to justify detention orders under the Internal Security Act, and have often set aside orders under the Emergency Regulations. I need mention only the *Hurley* case[8] and the *Nkwinti* case.[9] Such judgments would not have been given during the 1960 Emergency.

This is by no means to say that all is well and that we have reached the sunny uplands. While apartheid in the courts themselves has gone, one still unfortunately hears occasional reports of uncouth behaviour towards black practitioners by magistrates and prosecutors.

One may also ask whether the recent changes in judicial attitudes indicate anything more than a limited attempt to climb back to the standards of 1948. Is it simply that a number of liberal-minded judges have been prepared to tilt the balance a little towards individual rights? I think that it is far more than that. I believe that what I have tried to describe is a reflection in the courts of a profound change in South African society. I venture to say that this change can be dated from the events in Soweto in June 1976, and that since that date there has been a general acceptance of the fact that Verwoerdian apartheid had failed, even within the party that had created it. Nobody now doubts that apartheid is bound to go sooner or later. True, the basic structures of apartheid society are still in place – residential segregation, educational segregation and white political control. But even those who maintain this structure have lost confidence in it. Their excuses for maintaining it carry no inward conviction.

---

[6] *Komani NO v Bantu Affairs Administration Board, Peninsula Area* 1980(4) SA 448 (A).
[7] *Oos-Randse Administrasieraad v Rikhoto* 1983(3) SA 595 (A).
[8] *Minister of Law and Order v Hurley* 1986(3) SA 568 (A).
[9] *Nkwinti v Commissioner of Police* 1986(2) SA 421 (E).

This loss of confidence is widespread. One result has been a diminishing readiness, even among those who have been supporters of the government, to accept that the government automatically knows best; or that the security police are to be implicitly believed. Even in white society there is now a spirit of scepticism rather than subservience. It is this scepticism which is reflected in some of the judgments which I have mentioned. Judges may still apply the provisions of the Group Areas Act if they have to. As recently as 1981,[10] the Appellate Division refused to depart from the 1961 judgment in the *Lockhat* case,[11] in which the Appellate Division had held that the Group Areas Act must be read as impliedly permitting substantial inequality of treatment, even though the Act did not expressly do so. But it is inconceivable that any judge today could say, as Holmes JA did in 1961, that 'the Group Areas Act represents a colossal social experiment'.[12] And if he did, nobody would believe him.

III. CHANGES IN LEGAL PRACTICE

The period since 1976 has also seen great changes in the practice of the law. There are new forms of legal practice not previously known in this country. Employment law is the first in both volume and importance. It is a subject taught in the law schools and it has become a specialist branch of legal practice with a growing number of practitioners. This growth is obviously associated with the recognition of black trade unions in 1981 (a major landmark in the disintegration of apartheid) and the expansion of their economic power. Another form of legal practice which did not exist ten years ago is public interest law. This change can be precisely dated to the establishment of the Centre for Applied Legal Studies and the Legal Resources Centre in 1979. Both these bodies, apart from their other activities, have created law firms of a new sort. They consist of both advocates and attorneys who, while acting for individual clients, do so with the aim of protecting and vindicating the rights of whole communities and classes of people. In the nature of things, most of their clients come from the disadvantaged sections of the black population. These centres have attracted some of the ablest lawyers in the country. They have

[10] See *S v Adams, S v Werner* 1981 (1) SA 187 (A).
[11] *Lockhat v Minister of the Interior* 1961(2) SA 587 (A).
[12] Ibid, 602D.

provided the opportunity of legal careers perhaps more satisfying than careers in company or tax law even if, unfortunately, not quite as lucrative.

Another change, which is remarkable to those of us who were about in the 1950s and 1960s, is the vast increase in the volume of what I can broadly call civil rights litigation. During the past two years, attorneys and advocates throughout the country have brought numerous habeas corpus applications, applications for interdicts to stop ill-treatment of detained persons and proceedings to establish or protect the rights of prisoners. This is a far cry from the early 1960s, when only a handful of embattled attorneys[13] were prepared to take on political cases and, in particular, political criminal trials. Now, I understand, that has become a major area of competitive endeavour.

I have not yet mentioned what, to those of us who were in practice in those early years, must appear one of the greatest changes in the practice of law. That is the emergence of a body of black practitioners with the ability and the confidence to act in civil rights cases and political trials. This has been a positive achievement and not merely a natural development. It is an achievement because black practitioners have had to overcome the disadvantages of Bantu Education and tribal college law schools in order to qualify themselves for legal practice. (It is only very recently that black students have been entering the law schools of the open universities in any numbers.) There were other handicaps, also now largely overcome. I recall that in the early 1950s the first black member of the Johannesburg Bar was Mr Duma Nokwe. The then Minister of Bantu Affairs, Dr Verwoerd, refused to give him a permit to enable him to take chambers in the building which housed the Johannesburg Bar. What is more, his admission to the Bar common room was secured only against the opposition of a small but vocal and determined minority of the members of the Johannesburg Bar. Today, perhaps the leading civil rights advocate of South Africa is a black practitioner.[14] When he first came to the Johannesburg Bar, the law did not permit him to be a tenant of chambers in the centre of Johannesburg. When he first used to appear in the Appellate Division (which then, as now, had its seat in the Orange Free State province), it was illegal for him to stay in the Orange Free State overnight

---

[13] As distinct from advocates.
[14] In reference to Ismail Mohamed, later Chief Justice.

without a permit. I recall, too, that when, in the early 1970s, I was Chairman of the Johannesburg Bar Council, we were told by the owners of the licensed premises where we were to hold our Bar dinner that we had to have police permission if black members of the Bar were to attend. I remember interviewing a colonel of police whose main concern was to receive an assurance that there would be no dancing. All that is now history. Even the Pretoria Bar, that home of what I hope are lost causes, has, admittedly with much agony and recrimination, removed the colour bar from its constitution.

It is always pleasant to be able to point to positive advances, but, of course, they are not the whole story. Our legal and judicial system is still deeply flawed. The basic flaw has been stated time and again. It requires no original insight to see that, to the majority of those subject to the laws of this country, the law is not seen as a protection against injustice but as an oppressive force. It follows that the courts themselves are perceived by many as an integral part of an oppressive system, and as an alien institution.

In the criminal courts a black accused will ordinarily see a white prosecutor and a white magistrate or judge administering justice, often in a language which he does not understand well and which has to be interpreted to him, and – perhaps this is most important – applying a law which he and his community have had no say at all in making. Save in the few cases where adequate legal assistance is obtained, the law does not give the average black urban dweller protection against the host of insolent civil servants who control his life – on the contrary, the prosecutor and the magistrate are likely to be seen as simply another extension of the system of township managers, location superintendents and local authority officialdom.

IV. BLACK FEELINGS

It is not for me to speak for blacks, but one must surely be insensitive not to grasp the widespread feeling among blacks that, even in terms of the existing laws of the country, they do not get a fair deal in the courts. This is in part because of the factors which I have just mentioned. But it must also arise sometimes out of the vexed question of differences in sentences for what appears to be the same criminal offence. It is always difficult to make a true comparison between sentences in different cases. Cases may look similar yet the circumstances of the crime might be different; so may the circumstances of the accused. Nonetheless, there have been too many cases even in very recent times in which the race of either the accused or the victim seems to have played a part in the sentencing of the accused. It is not within the scope of this lecture to make a collection of such cases, but let me mention a few, some recent and some not so recent. Many years ago a group of young white men seriously assaulted a black man and gang-raped his wife. They were found guilty of rape, given a wholly suspended sentence and advised by the judge to join a club in order to give them something constructive to do in the evenings. A few years ago a number of white high school boys thought they would have a bit of fun with a black tramp found in their school grounds one night. The fun consisted in kicking him to death. The boys were found guilty of culpable homicide and their sentence was this: to spend all their weekends for one year working at a local hospital. There was the case of the white policeman who was given a paltry fine after he had knocked down a 'coloured' man, who died as a result of his fall. The very recent case of the white man who drove his car over a black woman in a Pretoria park must be fresh in everyone's memory. The judges and magistrates concerned had no doubt considered all the circumstances of these cases and may have had what they considered good reasons for the sentences. But as an advocate of more than thirty-five years' experience, I know, with an absolute certainty, that if in these cases the races of the victims and the accused had been reversed, sentences of such leniency could not possibly have been imposed.

A former judge once told me that one of the things he learned on the Bench was that he had no knowledge of the lives of black people, of their feelings, their loyalties or the pressures on them. He at least had the sensitivity and perception to understand this. The simple fact is that for the most part blacks do not participate in the administration of justice in South Africa, except passively. If this is so, the obvious solution seems to be to involve the black population actively in the administration of justice. What can we lawyers do to bring that about? But before one answers that question, another, more fundamental one arises. Is it at this stage worth making the effort?

This is a fundamental question for a number of reasons. In the first place, the basic legal structure of the country remains a structure of domination of black by white. It is a structure which is kept in place by an apparatus of security laws which give enormous powers to the executive and which place the narrowest limits on the jurisdiction of the courts to protect the individual against the exercise of that power. Even if every accused person or litigant had a lawyer, and even if every judge were a Centlivres or a Schreiner, the courts could not alter the fundamental realities of South African life. Only a radical political change could do that.

V. THE FUTURE

What conclusion this leads to must depend on one's view of the political future of South Africa. I have said that apartheid is bound to go sooner or later. If you believe that it will be so much later that nothing we do now can be relevant, it would be rational to leave everything to history. If you believe that a successful revolution will take place in the near future, you may think that the new revolutionary government will decide what legal system it wants. In that case, there would not be much point in tinkering with the present system. Such views cannot be shown to be wrong and may logically and comfortably justify a policy of inactivity. Certainly, to those who hope and believe a revolution is imminent, anything other than the revolution itself may be regarded as irrelevant. Indeed, if this is one's view, there would be no point in the meantime in attending a law school – you might be learning the wrong law.

However, I do not think that many people, whatever their political beliefs, really apply that logic. The first objection to it that I would raise is a general and practical one. Nobody can say how much time will pass before the present legal and constitutional system comes to an end. (After Sharpeville in 1960, some respected analysts gave it five years.) In the meantime, many people will live and die under the present system. Ordinary people are involved in litigation; they need and want lawyers to help them. Whatever the future, therefore, there seems to me to be an immediate moral and practical case for expanding the existing benefits of our legal system and for reducing its inequities as far as we can.

The second objection which I would raise against a policy of inactivity is a more personal one. I myself do not believe in either of the scenarios which I outlined above. I claim no special political expertise or insight, but that has never been a bar to political prophecy. I am going to use my privileged position as a lecturer to tell you how I see the future – whether I am optimistic, pessimistic or realistic is for you to judge. I believe that the conflict between black liberation movements and the South African government is one which both sides must ultimately realise cannot be won outright. A military victory against the formidable South African armed forces by black insurgents and black revolutionaries in the foreseeable future is hardly a real possibility. But the government's policy of pacification by a mixture of force and peripheral reforms is just as unlikely to succeed. If the conflict is to continue, the prospect is one of indefinite although limited violence against the forces of the state and eventually the white population. This violence would no doubt be reinforced by industrial action and internal boycotts. This will, in turn, be met by repression of an increasingly violent and unpleasant nature. This is likely to bring in its train a lengthening of the present period of conscription for young white men, more foreign disinvestment, and general decline in the economy and in the quality of life for nearly everyone. This prospect, however appalling, is not likely to lead either side into unconditional surrender. Reason therefore suggests that both sides will eventually see that a negotiated settlement is a necessity. A negotiated settlement would rationally include an agreed constitutional structure. One hopes that such a structure would include an independent judiciary and an independent legal profession. If that is not an entirely irrational hope, then it is surely worth using such time as is left to us to prove to the majority of the people of South Africa the value of those institutions, and to involve them actively in their workings.

There is much that the legal profession can still do to this end.

In the first place, we must do all in our power to develop the concept of law as a protection against power, even under the present system. This means developing and expanding the work already done by the Legal Resources Centre and the Centre for Applied Legal Studies, and, more recently, by the Black Lawyers Association. Legal services must be provided not only in political cases, but as widely as possible for blacks caught up in the mess of regulations which still exists notwithstanding the abolition of influx control. Nor is it government alone against which the protection of the law is needed. Unscrupulous hire purchase dealers and bogus insurance companies are only two examples of that part of the private sector (as it is now fashionably called) whose business is to exploit the less sophisticated members of the black population. Every time one of these enterprising businessmen is forced to disgorge by means of legal process (even if it be only a lawyer's letter), the image of the law as a protector is enhanced. The same thing happens when a lawyer assists a wrongfully dismissed domestic servant to claim a month's wages in lieu of notice. It may be objected that there are not enough lawyers in South Africa to do this work. I shall refer in a moment to the need to expand the legal profession. But the need for legal services of the type which I have mentioned calls for new and flexible forms of legal practice. A major development has been the establishment of the community advice office staffed not by lawyers but by members of the community who have received some basic instruction in such matters as rights to pensions or to unemployment insurance and rights under township regulations. They are able to assist members of their community in dealing with the simpler legal problems which constantly arise in their lives. When more difficult problems arise, the advice office will refer them to a qualified lawyer. There are already in the Transvaal alone some 25 advice offices of this type which operate with the assistance of the Legal Resources Centre. There is an obvious need for funds to establish more advice offices, to train those who work in them and to provide legal advice for them when it is needed.

Another source of legal services of a similar kind is the university law clinic, run by law students under the supervision of a member of the faculty. The University of the Witwatersrand established the first of these clinics. Many other universities now have them. They, too, provide legal advice at elementary level. The University of Natal Law School has gone even further. It has a programme, picturesquely called 'Street Law', which takes lawyers to high schools, particularly in black communities, to teach that there are such things as legal rights as well as legal obligations and that law is something which can be used as well as merely endured.

VI. MORE BLACK LAWYERS

If these developments are to be successful, the overriding necessity is for a really substantial increase in the number of black advocates and attorneys. This is urgent, but not easy to achieve in short order. I have already mentioned the effort needed to overcome the disadvantages of Bantu Education – a system designed to ensure that there would be as few as possible well-qualified black professional men and women to spoil Dr Verwoerd's vision of the future.

The law graduates of the tribal colleges, through no fault of their own, are seldom adequately qualified to go straight into private practice. Graduates of those colleges who go on to do an LLB at this university or other open universities often require bridging courses. An LLB degree may therefore be a long undertaking and for black students often impossible without maintenance over and above the cost of tuition. Many bursaries are available, but there are never enough.

The problems do not end at the university. In present economic conditions it is not easy for any students, white or black, to obtain employment in law firms. Thus, the number of black advocates has grown only very slowly. For example, the Johannesburg Bar has about 350 members. As far as I know, only about a dozen of them are black. I believe that Bar Councils should actively recruit well-qualified young black lawyers to their branch of the profession.

Most of the suggestions I have made require the raising of funds. In the present climate of opinion here and abroad it should not be impossible to do so. It would be money well spent. I can think of nothing which would more thoroughly and beneficially change the substance as well as the appearance of the administration of justice in our courts than to see large numbers of competent black practitioners regularly appearing in all our courts on behalf of black clients. The courts would lose their alien appearance to the black litigant or accused. It would influence and educate the white prosecutors, magistrates and judges who will for the most part continue to fill those positions. I am sanguine enough to believe that even the discrepancies in sentencing which I referred to earlier would become markedly less frequent if judicial officers had the daily experience of meeting black professional men and women in their courts.

This lecture has concentrated on the place of lawyers in our changing country; that is, on one small segment of our society. I think it is as important as any, because a country without an independent legal profession would be a doomed country. That is too large a topic to expand on now.

The law was a profession in which Ernie Wentzel could give practical expression to his ideals. I hope that there will be many young lawyers of all races who will follow the calling of the law in his fashion.

5

*The Ethics of Advocacy**

~

I MUST RELUCTANTLY confess that I have been a working advocate for over 50 years – in South Africa, England, and, occasionally, some other jurisdictions. That presumably is why the leader of this circuit invited me to give one of this series of lectures on advocacy. Unfortunately, the longer I go on in this profession the less I have to say about what is sometimes called the art and sometimes, more modestly, the technique of advocacy. So I hope that nobody has come here this evening expecting hints on advocacy. There are some basic techniques that can certainly be taught with advantage to young and not-so-young advocates. But in the end your advocacy will be a reflection of your own character and personality, and your own particular talents. Each one of us in the law has seen in a courtroom some counsel whom we particularly admire, whom we think of as a truly great advocate. But that does not mean that one should try to imitate his or her style of advocacy. It cannot be done, and the attempt may be disastrous.

There are, after all, many different styles of advocacy, both national and individual. If I had to classify the English style, I would describe it as idiosyncratic. Recently a retired chancery judge in London was heard to say that in his time at the Chancery Bar they did not take much account of advocacy. In fact, he said, even audibility was regarded as an affectation. On the other hand, there was Sir Hartley Shawcross QC. Appearing in an appeal presided over by that formidable Lord Chief Justice, Lord Goddard, he began by saying, 'My Lords, there are three points

* This is the text of a talk given at the Inner Temple in January 2003 as one of a series of talks on The Art of Advocacy organised by the South Eastern Circuit of the Bar of England and Wales.

in this appeal. One is hopeless, one is arguable and one is unanswerable.' To which Lord Goddard said impatiently, 'Sir Hartley, just give us your best point.' 'Oh no,' said Sir Hartley, 'I don't propose to tell your Lordships which is which.'

Those are illustrations, not recommendations.

If I could not speak about the art or technique of advocacy, what was there to say on the subject? I should like to venture a few remarks not so much on the Rules of the Bar (which we are all supposed to know), but rather on the ethical basis of our profession. It is a profession (and not the only profession) whose practitioners face ethical problems. Some of them are old chestnuts. Most lawyers at some time in their career are asked by friends (or critics) 'How can you appear for someone whom you know is guilty?' That is not generally a very difficult question. Our Codes of Conduct tells us what we must or may do if a client confesses guilt to us but still wishes to be defended. We may not make any suggestion to a witness which we know to be untrue; we may not suggest to the judge or the jury that the crime was committed by someone else; we may not put the client in the witness box to give evidence which we know by his own confession to be false. But we may put the prosecution to strict proof of the guilt of the accused and may argue that the proof is insufficient. If the client is not prepared to proceed on that basis, we must withdraw from the defence.

That is plain enough, and in any event, it does not often arise in the real world. When do we 'know' that a client is guilty? I did many criminal cases in South Africa, and I can recall only one instance where a client told me that he was guilty. He explained in detail how he had committed an ingenious fraud. It then became clear that he had no intention of pleading guilty and he told me the equally ingenious defence he was preparing to put up. I explained that on that basis I could not appear for him. He was a quick student. He took the point, thanked me and went off with his silent solicitor – no doubt to another advocate, with whom he was presumably more circumspect.

That is not to say that every problem of professional conduct has a simple solution. It is a trite proposition that counsel must not mislead the court by word or deed and must not suppress what ought to be disclosed. But what ought to be disclosed? A few years ago, in an English case, *Vernon v Bosley*,[1] a plaintiff who

---

[1] [1999] QB 18.

had witnessed the drowning of his two children in an accident caused by the negligence of the defendants obtained substantial damages for post-traumatic stress disorder and serious mental illness. The findings in favour of the plaintiff were based on the evidence of a consultant psychiatrist and a trained psychologist. Now it happened that there had been quite separate contested proceedings between the plaintiff and his wife in a different court, with different counsel, over the custody of their surviving children. In those proceedings the same psychiatrist and the same psychologist had given very different evidence for the husband, supporting his claim for custody, saying that his condition had improved dramatically, and giving a prognosis far more optimistic than that which they gave in the personal injury action. The husband's legal advisers in the personal injury action learnt of this contradictory evidence of their own witnesses only after the close of evidence in their case, but before the judge had given his judgment. They advised that this contradictory evidence need not be disclosed to the other side, or to the judge. So the judge made his substantial award of damages in ignorance of it. The defendants somehow later found out about the evidence in the custody case and appealed to the Court of Appeal. They challenged the propriety of the conduct of the plaintiff's lawyers in failing to make disclosure of what they had learned. They argued that the new evidence ought to have been disclosed and that the failure to do so amounted to misleading the court. There were three judgments in the Court of Appeal. Stuart-Smith LJ said that the counsel in the personal injury case should have advised his client that disclosure should be made. If the client had not agreed to that course, counsel should have withdrawn from the case; but, he said, it was not for counsel to make the disclosure himself contrary to the client's wishes. (What good counsel's withdrawal would have done once the hearing was over and the judge had reserved judgment Stuart-Smith LJ did not say.) Thorpe LJ, on the other hand, said that, whatever his client's attitude, counsel had a positive duty to disclose the relevant material to his opponent and to the judge. This duty to the court was paramount. But Evans LJ said that, once the evidence in the personal injury case was closed, there was no duty on counsel to make any disclosure at all. So, even on what may have seemed a relatively simple professional question, an experienced Court of Appeal spoke with three voices.

The Bar Council is constantly asked to rule on such specific questions of proper professional conduct. They come up in the advocacy exercises which are part of training for newly qualified barristers. What I want to consider is a more general subject – the moral underpinning of the profession which we practise, that is, the profession of representing clients in court. You might think that a learned profession which has been lawfully practised at least since the days of the Roman Republic should have no need to examine its collective conscience. But there are old and nagging questions which, however often answered, do not seem to go away.

In one of the best-known passages in Boswell's *Life of Johnson,* Boswell (himself a practising Scottish advocate) asks: 'But what do you think of supporting a cause which you know to be bad?' Dr Johnson's robust reply was: 'Sir, you do not know it to be good or bad until the judge determines it.'

But Dr Johnson did not dispose of the question, which still lingers more than two hundred years on. His is a good enough answer if the cause is a matter of pure law, or if its goodness or badness can only be determined after all the witnesses have been heard.

As I have already noted, short of a confession by his client, counsel cannot be said actually to 'know' that his client is guilty, whatever counsel may suspect. In the strict sense of the word (which was Dr Johnson's sense), we may not 'know' that our client's cause is bad. But there are many states of mind which are short of knowledge but which still provoke Boswell's question. Many of us practising lawyers must have had the client who stoutly professes his innocence or good faith, but whom we, with our experience, our observation of the client in conference, and our knowledge of the facts of the case, just do not believe. We may warn the client that the judge or the jury are not likely to believe him, but the client may persist in his version of events and may insist on his case going forward. We are in no position in such a case to prevent him from giving evidence. We cannot assert that his evidence will be perjured. He may even persuade the court to accept his evidence. Yet we in our hearts and minds remain convinced that his case is a false one.

Take another case. Our client has in law a good case; the facts and the law support him. He is not acting out of malice, but we view his cause with distaste. We see it as a bad cause not because of the client's character, or his politics or reputation (all of which are irrelevant), but because we believe that the action we are instructed to bring is oppressive, or in our view contrary to the public interest. For example, a financial institution instructs us to bring a well-founded suit which will result in the ruin of a small shopkeeper and his family. A property-owner has the right to evict from his land a community which will be left homeless and instructs us to take steps to do so. Or the client is a developer who is asserting a good legal right which we know will result in the destruction of the amenities of a neighbourhood. Or we may be briefed in a criminal case for a client who has a good legal defence but whose conduct we regard as morally indefensible.

Surely a modern Boswell would be entitled to classify those as bad causes and to put his question to us?

One theoretically possible answer must immediately be rejected. It is not an option to refuse to act in such cases. That is the cab-rank rule. There may be personal reasons why a particular barrister may refuse to handle a particular case, eg a conflict of interest or a relationship to one of the parties, but the duty of the Bar as a whole to afford representation in the type of case which I have described is inescapable. Whatever a lawyer's personal reason may be for declining a brief, it may not be because he thinks that the cause is a bad one in the sense which I have tried to illustrate. It is a fundamental constitutional principle of any country which would describe itself as free that every person accused of a crime should be entitled to legal representation. That greatest of English advocates, Thomas Erskine, in his defence of Tom Paine, addressed the court in words which still resound after two hundred years:[2]

> From the moment that any advocate can be permitted to say that he will or will not stand between the Crown and the subject arraigned in the court where he daily sits to practise, from that moment the liberties of England are at an end.

Rhetorical as that may seem, I do not consider it to be an exaggeration. During the long years of apartheid in South Africa, I believe that one of the things which kept the flame of liberty flickering was that opponents of the apartheid regime charged with offences including high treason were able to find members of the Bar to defend them with such skill as they had and with vigour. This was not because they necessarily sympathised with the aims or methods of the accused, but rather because they recognised their professional duty to take on those cases.

This duty of the Bar extends to civil cases. It cannot be doubted

[2] *R v Paine* (1792) 22 State Trials 412.

that the right to counsel is one of the principles of fundamental justice in civil actions as well as in criminal prosecutions. It hardly needs stating that the right to counsel would be of little value if the Bar did not recognise a moral and professional duty to make its services available without regard to any consideration of whether the client's cause be categorised as good or bad.

Some years ago Lord Pearce, in the House of Lords, restated this principle more prosaically than Erskine, but just as forcefully:[3]

> It is easier, pleasanter and more advantageous professionally for barristers to represent or defend those who are decent and reasonable and likely to succeed in their action or their defence than those who are unpleasant, unreasonable, disreputable and have an apparently hopeless case. Yet it would be tragic if our legal system came to provide no reputable defenders, representatives or advisers for the latter.

Given our cab-rank rule, what can be the present significance of what I may call the Boswell question? It remains a live question, but I would venture to rephrase it, in this way: how should an advocate, as a member of an honourable profession, conduct himself or herself in a cause which, on rational grounds, he or she firmly believes to be unmeritorious or morally objectionable?

I emphasise, in passing, the words 'honourable profession'. Nowadays one hears it said that we barristers must realise that we constitute a service industry; and that in a competitive world we must market ourselves competitively. Nonetheless, I believe that we are still a profession and not merely a business. As Lord Devlin pointed out nearly 50 years ago, in a case concerning not lawyers but architects,[4] many activities which in the business world are regarded as laudable examples of enterprise may by the rules of a profession be considered an offence. The old rules against advertising and against undercutting our colleagues have undergone considerable relaxation, but the distinction between a profession and a business still, I hope, remains. Some things permitted in the business world are not open to us.

I return to my rephrased question. One response, as robust and as simple as Dr Johnson's, is that, whether the cause be good or bad, once the brief has been accepted, the advocate has a single duty – his duty to his client. This was stated in terms of unsurpassed eloquence and power by a great English legal

---

[3] *Rondel v Worsley* [1969] 1 AC 191, 275.
[4] *Hughes v Architects Registration Council* [1957] 2 QB 550.

figure, one of Erskine's successors as a leading counsel and later Lord Chancellor, Henry Brougham. In 1820 he defended Queen Caroline against the charge of adultery brought against her by her husband, King George IV. The trial was before the House of Lords. In addressing the Lords, Brougham described the duty of counsel in these words:[5]

> An advocate, by the sacred duty which he owes his client, knows in the discharge of that office but one person in the world – that client and none other. To save that client by all expedient means, to protect that client at all hazards and costs to all others, and amongst others to himself, is the highest and most unquestioned of his duties; and he must not regard the alarm, the suffering, the torment, the destruction, which he may bring upon any other. Nay, separating even the duties of a patriot from those of an advocate, and casting them, if need be, to the wind, he must go on reckless of the consequences, if his fate it should unhappily be, to involve his country in confusion for his client's protection.

That statement of the duty of the advocate was not wholly endorsed by the leaders of the profession. Some even thought it outrageous, but Lord Brougham, as he became, never departed from it. It has unfortunately and, I think, wrongly been invoked as demonstrating an absence of any moral standards in the advocates' profession. One of the critics of our profession who did invoke it for that very purpose was able to match Brougham in eloquence.

In 1838, Benjamin Disraeli was a young Member of Parliament. Thirty years were to pass before he became Prime Minister of England. In that year of 1838, following a parliamentary election, a petition was brought to unseat one of the successful candidates. Disraeli himself was not a party to the proceedings, or in any way concerned in them, but in the course of the court hearing a Mr Austin, counsel for the petitioner, had referred to Disraeli in what Disraeli took to be insulting and defamatory terms. What Mr Austin had said in court was, of course, absolutely privileged: Mr Austin could not be sued for defamation. So Disraeli published a letter in the newspapers. It is worth quoting at length, as a salutary reminder of an opinion of our profession which some hold to this day. Disraeli began by indicating that he would have taken action in court but, he said, he had been: [6]

---

[5] *The Queen's Case* (1820) 2 Brod & Bing 284.
[6] This passage and those quoted below are taken from WT Moneypenny, *The Life of Benjamin Disraeli* (John Murray, London, 1912) vol II, ch II.

assured that Mr Austin, by the custom of his profession, was authorised
to make any statement from his brief which he was prepared to
substantiate, or to attempt to substantiate . . . I take the earliest
opportunity of declaring, and in a manner the most unequivocal that
the statement of the learned gentleman is utterly false.

I am informed that it is quite useless to expect from Mr Austin any
satisfaction for those impertinent calumnies, because Mr Austin is
a member of an honourable profession, the first principle of whose
practice appears to be that they may say anything provided they be
paid for it. The privilege of circulating falsehoods with impunity is
delicately described as doing your duty towards your client, which
appears to be a very different process to doing your duty towards
your neighbour. This may be the usage of Mr Austin's profession, but,
for my part, it appears to me to be nothing better than a disgusting
and intolerable tyranny, and I, for one, shall not bow to it in silence.

I therefore repeat that the statement of Mr Austin was false, and,
inasmuch as he never attempted to substantiate it, I conclude that it
was, on his side, but the blustering artifice of a rhetorical hireling,
availing himself of the vile licence of a loose-tongued lawyer, not
only to make a statement which was false, but to make it with a
consciousness of its falsehood.

Disraeli hoped to provoke a challenge to a duel. Instead, Austin
had Disraeli cited for contempt. Disraeli was forced by the judges
to make an apology in open court. It must be the least grovelling
apology in history. After formally apologising to Austin, he said
he feared that he had really been brought to court not so much
for an offence against the law as an offence against lawyers. He
expressed the belief

that there is in the principles on which the practice of the Bar
in England is based a taint of arrogance; which is the necessary
consequence of the possession and the exercise of irresponsible
power . . . I confess that I myself have imbibed an opinion that it
is the duty of a counsel to his client to assist him by all possible
means, just or unjust, and even to commit if necessary, a crime for
his assistance or extrication. This may be an outrageous opinion,

he said, 'but, my Lords, it is not my own.' He then quoted the
passage from Brougham's speech which I have already read out.
Brougham by then was an ex-Lord Chancellor, so this quotation
was something of a knockout blow. Disraeli, in a final thrust,
appealed to the Bench to shield him 'from the vengeance of an
irritated and powerful profession'.

The Attorney-General wisely accepted this dubious apology as 'ample' and no sentence was passed. One is grateful not to have had the experience of crossing Disraeli. Of course the profession was irritated. Disraeli's attack was exaggerated, and it was unfair to Brougham. Brougham did not say that it could ever be the duty of counsel to commit a crime. Nor was it true that the ethics of the Bar permitted an advocate to utter a deliberate falsehood. It was not permissible then or now, and I do not think that Brougham was saying that it was. When Brougham spoke of the duty to save the client by all means and expedients, I do not doubt that he meant honest means and expedients. Yet we cannot simply dismiss Disraeli's harsh criticism of our profession. When we speak in court, we do enjoy great latitude and great privileges. I fear that these advantages do sometimes lead to a professional arrogance, and, especially in the heat of battle, to an excessive licence in attacking the parties or witnesses on the other side. I am uncomfortably conscious in the course of a long practice of having (only occasionally, I hope) transgressed in this way. It is a danger which confronts all of us who call ourselves trial lawyers. Our duties to all our clients, good or bad, must be limited by ethical considerations. Brougham's statement that we need take no account of 'the alarm, the suffering, the torment, the destruction' we may bring upon others is not to be taken literally, without qualification.

I shall return to this point later. But first there is another (not unrelated) aspect of professional practice especially worth stressing. The advocate should not identify himself or herself with the client's cause. The advocate speaks for the client in court, as a professional representative, not as a partisan. The corollary strictly applied in England and Wales as part of our Code of Conduct is that it is highly improper for an advocate to assert either to a judge or a jury any personal belief in the rightness or justice of the client's cause. It is equally improper to make any such assertion to the media outside court. In recent years it has become common after some high-profile case to see and hear on television the solicitor for one of the parties either protesting the client's innocence or (depending on the outcome) announcing that justice has triumphed. This is apparently permissible for solicitors. I trust that the Bar Council will be firm in ensuring that members of the Bar do not follow that practice. As a barrister, you are the legal representative of your client, not the client's general agent or spokesman or public relations adviser. This clear limitation on the role of the advocate is an important aspect of the independence of the Bar. It includes a degree of independence even from the client. It is this rule which provides an honourable basis on which we can give our professional services to a client whose integrity we doubt and whose conduct we disapprove of. Yet another nineteenth-century Lord Chancellor (this time Lord Herschell) said, in words which may today seem pompous, but which are nonetheless relevant to our consideration of the ethical basis of our profession:[7]

> It is only by keeping this rule [ie of not identifying oneself with the client's cause] constantly in mind, and by a strict adherence to it in practice, that the risk of injury to the moral character of the advocate by his seeking to convince others by arguments which have not brought conviction to his own mind can be avoided.

Another English judge said[8] that '[t]here is an honourable way of defending the worst of cases'. I would add that there is an honourable way of prosecuting and defending all cases, the best as well as the worst. In either case, there are things which, even if not illegal, an honourable advocate would not do – like suggesting to a client what would be a good defence, or attempting to play on what are, or are believed to be, the racial or other prejudices of the jury or the judge, or deliberately employing certain tactics. Let me take an example, unfortunately not entirely hypothetical. Suppose you have a client to whom money is no object. He suggests that if the case is drawn out as long as possible the other side will be battered into submission. This tactic may be furthered by opening the case at inordinate length, reading out every possible document. I hope you will all agree that no honourable advocate would do that, even if a weak judge were to permit it. So the basic answer to the Boswell question is that the advocate must conduct himself in a bad cause as in a good cause. He must represent the client resolutely and <u>honourably</u> within the limits of the law.

When it comes to 'the honourable way', there is one aspect of practice which I have found peculiarly difficult. The Code of Conduct of the English Bar states that a barrister conducting proceedings in Court:

[7] *The Rights and Duties of an Advocate* (Wm Hodge & Co, Glasgow, 1890) 11.
[8] Hannen P in *Smith v Smith* (1882) 7 PD 84, 89.

must not suggest that a victim, witness or other person is guilty of crime, fraud or misconduct or make any defamatory aspersion on the conduct of any other person or attribute to another person the crime or conduct of which his lay client is accused unless such allegations go to a matter in issue (including the credibility of the witness) which is material to his lay client's case and *which appear to him to be supported by reasonable grounds.*

This, of course, qualifies Brougham's statement that in doing our duty to our client we must not regard the suffering or torment we may bring on any other person. But that rule does not allay our doubts.

Consider this case. Your client's version of events may require you to cross-examine a witness who gives a materially different version damaging to your client. Your client's own evidence would under this professional rule constitute reasonable grounds for impugning the witness and thus permit you to challenge the veracity of the witness. The Code of Conduct certainly permits you to challenge that witness. Indeed, it is ordinarily your duty to do so. But, having seen and heard that witness, and understanding the facts of the case, you are convinced, however contrary to your client's instructions, that the witness is an honest witness giving truthful evidence. Would you still find it morally permissible to cross-examine so as to suggest that the witness is a liar? How far do you feel able to go in such a case? Anyone with long trial experience has faced this problem. I have, on several occasions; and all I shall say is that, looking back, I am not satisfied that my judgment was invariably right.

This situation was graphically illustrated in Trollope's great legal novel, *Orley Farm.*[9] A young and idealistic barrister is junior counsel for a lady who is the defendant in a perjury prosecution arising out of a disputed will. A simple, ill-educated serving woman, who was one of the witnesses to the will, is called by the prosecution. Her straightforward evidence contradicts that of the barrister's client and is seriously damaging to her. To the young barrister it is plain beyond dispute that this witness is giving her evidence with complete honesty. Chaffanbrass QC, the elderly leader who cross-examines her, also sees this, but that does not deter him. As the author puts it: 'He could not make a fool of her, and therefore he would make her out to be a rogue.'

[9] First published in serial form in 1861 and in book form (by Chapman & Hall) in 1862.

At the end of the cross-examination, the author continues:

[The QC] knew well enough that she [the witness] had spoken nothing but the truth. But had he so managed that the truth might be made to look like falsehood . . .? If he had done that he had succeeded in the occupation of his life.

The young barrister is appalled at his leader's cross-examination and cannot conceal his distaste He thereby incurs the scorn of his leader. At the end of the trial (the whole of which makes enthralling reading), the old QC says to the younger man sarcastically: 'You are too great for this kind of work . . . If a man undertakes a duty he should do it . . . especially if he takes money for it.'

Which of them was right? I content myself with suggesting that *Orley Farm* is a novel which every barrister should read.

I am conscious that, to most of the questions I have raised, I have been able to give no clear answer. You may be thinking that my reformulation of the Boswell question and my examples of bad causes were too bland. There are bad causes and bad causes. What if a client comes to counsel with a cause which seems not merely unappealing or unmeritorious, not merely contrary to some view of the public good, but which is utterly revolting to counsel's conscience? Whatever the general rule requiring counsel to provide their services to clients willing and able to pay their fees, are there not occasions when counsel should be entitled to follow his conscience and refuse to act?

There were cases like that in South Africa where counsel were briefed by the former government in cases designed to enforce the apartheid laws. I was, of course, not on the government's list of counsel, and was never asked to act for the government in such a case. There were fortunately, or unfortunately, any number of pro-apartheid members of the Bar who would take on those cases without, apparently, any qualm of conscience. The rules of conduct of the South African Bar included the cab-rank rule. The issue never arose for me. If it had arisen, I believe that I and many other advocates would have been unable to comply with the cab-rank rule. Perhaps no rule of conduct can be an absolute rule. There may be times, fortunately rare, when one's own conscience rather than the general rule must govern one's conduct.

I return to the words of Lord Brougham. Properly understood, they are rather splendid. 'To save that client by all expedient means, to protect that client at all hazards and costs to all others, and among others to himself.' That phrase 'to himself' is the key

to the whole passage. What Lord Brougham was asserting was
not a licence to lie and cheat. What he was asserting was that the
highest qualities demanded of an advocate are independence and
courage in defence of the client. The duty to show those qualities
to the best of our abilities remains. Courage and independence
sometimes entail standing up to a hostile bench – the annals of
the Bar record many examples of that. But courage and independence mean more than that. What Lord Brougham was saying was
that, in accepting a brief and in pursuing the lawful interests
of the client, we must put aside all consideration of pleasing or
displeasing others or of benefiting or harming ourselves. What you
say or do in court may displease powerful interests – a government, a trade union, a corporation with much legal business at its
disposal, an influential section of the community. It may be unwelcome to another of your important clients. It may offend your
friends, colleagues or perhaps even your own family. It may harm
your career. All such considerations, Brougham is telling us, must
be put aside. That may be an ideal not all of us can attain. But
it is an ideal we should all strive for. And, I would add, the duty
which Lord Brougham was describing is an intensely personal
one. You may take advice from your colleagues, but once you
are in court your conduct is your own responsibility, yours alone.
Three of the most important of our Rules of Conduct embody Lord
Brougham's great statement.

Rule 303 states:

A barrister
(a) must promote and protect fearlessly and by all proper and lawful
means the lay client's best interests and do so without regard to
his own interests or to any consequences to himself or to any other
person (including any professional client or other intermediary or
another barrister).

Rule 306 states:

A barrister is individually and personally responsible for his own
conduct and for his professional work: he must exercise his own
personal judgment in all his professional activities.

Rule 307 states:

A barrister must not:
(a) permit his absolute independence integrity and freedom from
external pressures to be compromised.

That is one reason why we are all sole practitioners, and why the Bar has never permitted partnerships. No other profession requires of its members so principled an approach to its professional duties.

Forty years after his defence of Queen Caroline, Lord Brougham made a speech at a Bar dinner in London. He ended it in these words:[10]

> In this country the administration of justice depends principally on the purity of the judges; but next on the prudence, the discretion and the courage of the advocate. No greater misfortune can befall the administration of justice than an infringement of the independence of the Bar or the failure of courage in our advocates.

This is as true in the twenty-first century as it was in the nineteenth. It is what gives our profession its unique value in our society and what ultimately justifies its continued existence.

~

---

[10] Featured in (1864) 40 *The Law Times* 16–18.

6

*Freedom of Speech: Is it the Primary Right?**

~

I. INTRODUCTION

THE TITLE OF this article is not intended to disparage the
value of freedom of speech in a modern democratic society.
The right freely and publicly to criticise the institutions of
government, the conduct of public affairs whether by the executive
or Parliament, the freedom, indeed, to criticise the performance
of the judiciary – that right is one of the glories of the unwritten
constitution of this country. Its importance is constantly and forcefully emphasised in our highest courts. In one of the Spycatcher
cases, Lord Bridge of Harwich said that the right to freedom of
speech is one of the fundamental freedoms essential to a free
society.[1] In the same case, Lord Oliver quoted Blackstone's statement that the liberty of the press is essential to the nature of
a free state.[2] More recently, Lord Goff of Chieveley, observing
that he could see no inconsistency between English law and the
European Convention on Human Rights in relation to freedom of
speech, added: 'This is scarcely surprising, since we may pride
ourselves on the fact that freedom of speech has existed in this
country perhaps as long as, if not longer than, it has existed in
any other country in the world.'[3]

Nor am I myself likely to underrate the value of free speech,
having spent the greater part of my professional life under an

---

* This was the 19th annual Francis Mann lecture, given at Lincoln's Inn in October
1995. Judge Stephen Schwebel, the then Vice-President of the International Court of
Justice, was in the chair.

[1] *Attorney-General v Guardian Newspapers Ltd* [1987] 1 WLR 1248, 1286.
[2] Ibid, 1320.
[3] *Attorney-General v Guardian Newspapers Ltd (No 2)* [1990] 1 AC 109, 283.

authoritarian government which, while not suppressing political criticism either on public platforms or in the press, nonetheless passed laws which grossly violated the common law traditions of free speech. Mention of a few cases will suggest the atmosphere of the period. In one of them, the editor and the reporter of a leading daily newspaper were convicted of a new criminal offence of negligently publishing incorrect information about conditions in prisons. In another, a law professor had conducted an opinion survey among a number of South African judges and barristers, asking the question whether the race of either the accused or the victim was a factor which influenced verdicts and sentences in criminal cases. He published the results in the *South African Law Journal*, including the fact that a fair percentage of both judges and advocates had answered in the affirmative. He was prosecuted for contempt of court and acquitted only on the grounds that he had not the subjective intention to bring the courts into contempt.[4] The same professor (a good lawyer, but one not apt to learn from experience) subsequently made a public speech in which he urged judges not to give credence to the evidence of prosecution witnesses if (as was often the case in political trials) they had been brought to court after long detention in police custody. This time he was indeed convicted.[5] It was some time before newspapers were again prepared to investigate conditions in prisons or the racial element in criminal prosecutions. So I am, I think, unlikely to undervalue freedom of speech. It is a right which should never be taken for granted. That is why it was proper to test in the courts of England the validity of the regulation which prohibited the broadcasting not of the opinions or the words but merely of the voices of members of unlawful organisations – although I may be forgiven for regarding this case[6] as being at the luxury end of the human rights spectrum.

II. IS FREEDOM OF SPEECH THE PRIMARY RIGHT?

What is meant by asking whether freedom of speech is the 'primary right'? A primary right is here used to mean a right which is not merely described as 'fundamental' but which is assumed to take precedence over other rights or interests. Neither

[4] *State v van Niekerk* 1970 (3) SA 655.
[5] *State v van Niekerk (2)* 1972 (3) SA 711.
[6] *R v Home Secretary, ex p Brind* [1991] 1 AC 696.

in English common law nor in most constitutional bills of rights is there to be found any formal hierarchy of rights, but in certain countries and at certain times some rights seem to be favoured above others. This is nothing new. For Blackstone, it was the right of property. 'There is nothing,' said Blackstone, 'which so generally strikes the imagination and engages the affections of mankind, as the right of property.'[7] In the United States, the Supreme Court has disavowed any hierarchy of constitutional rights, but I believe nonetheless that freedom of speech and of the press is in fact the primary right in this sense. A similar, if more limited, development is now to be seen in Australia. In the United States, the First Amendment to the Constitution provides that 'Congress shall make no law abridging the freedom of speech or of the press'. The Commonwealth of Australia has a written constitution, but it contains no bill of rights – the framers, it is understood, deliberately decided against one. The High Court of Australia has, however, recently discerned in the Australian Constitution an entrenched freedom of public discussion of political matters.[8] This freedom is implied as being essential to the system of representative democracy established by the Constitution. During the past four years, a number of statutes and rules of common law in Australia have in fact been held by the High Court to be unconstitutional as being in conflict with this implied term.[9]

There are good historical and political reasons for the American deference to First Amendment rights, beginning with the successful campaign against the Sedition Act of 1798. In any event, the choice was one for the American courts to make, and it seems to have commanded broad acceptance from both conservative and liberal justices in the United States. As to Australia, an outsider's mild surprise at the laying bare, after 90 years, of an unexpressed fundamental right in the Constitution cannot temper his admiration for the ingeniously reasoned process of discovery.

In England, freedom of speech, important though it is, is not the primary right in the same sense. There are those who think it ought to be. It should, of course, at once be made clear that, notwithstanding the 'primacy' of the right of freedom of speech in

---

[7] W Blackstone, *Commentaries on the Laws of England*, vol 11, 2.

[8] *Nationwide News Pty Limited v Wills* (1992) 177 CLR 1; *Australian Capital Television Pty Ltd and Others v The Commonwealth of Australia* (1992) 177 CLR 106.

[9] Ibid; see also *Theophanous v Herald and Weekly Times Ltd* (1994) 68 AJLR 713; *Stephens v West Australian Newspapers Ltd* (1994) 68 AJLR 765. See also T Jones, 'Freedom of Political Communication in Australia' (1996) 45 *International & Comparative Law Quarterly* 392.

some countries, in no constitution is the right absolute. Freedom of speech and of the press is always to be balanced against other legitimate interests. In some constitutional instruments, the balancing of the right of free speech against other interests is expressly provided for. In the Canadian Charter of Rights, among the fundamental rights is the freedom of speech and of the press. This, however, like other rights, is subject to section 1 of the Charter, which permits such reasonable limitations on Charter Rights 'as can be demonstrably justified in a free and democratic society'. Similarly, the new South African Constitution entrenches as a fundamental right freedom of speech and of the press,[10] but it permits the limitation of fundamental rights provided that such limitation is 'justifiable in an open and democratic society based on freedom and equality'.[11] Article 5 of the German Basic Law provides that the right of free expression may be limited for the protection of the citizen's right to personal respect. Under Article 10 of the European Convention on Human Rights the right to freedom of expression is subject to such restrictions as are prescribed by law and are necessary in a democratic society in the interest of, among other things, the protection of morals, the protection of the reputations or rights of others, or for maintaining the authority and impartiality of the judiciary.

As already stated, Lord Goff found no difference between the right of freedom of speech in the European Convention and the right under English common law. In all these systems a balancing is called for, or, rather, a weighing; in any particular case, the scales must come down on one side or another.

III. WHERE FREEDOM OF SPEECH
CONFLICTS WITH OTHER RIGHTS

In English courts freedom of speech may have to be weighed against other legally recognised rights, such as the right to reputation, the right to a fair trial, or the right to confidentiality. I stress a 'legally recognised right', for if a litigant seeks to set against freedom of speech some interest not recognised by English law (such as privacy) there is nothing to put into the balance. Thus, in 1994 the Court of Appeal refused to prevent a television broadcast of a programme which would have exposed a young child to

---

[10] Constitution of the Republic of South Africa Act, No 200 of 1993, s 15.
[11] Ibid, s 33.

harmful publicity.[12] Hoffmann LJ, in an illuminating judgment, explained that the desire to avoid intrusive publicity was not an interest to which at present English law gave protection. Outside the category of recognised rights or any new ones enacted by Parliament, there was 'no question of balancing freedom of speech against other interests. It is a trump card which always wins.'[13] (This last statement is sometimes quoted out of its context.) So it is in the context of conflicts between freedom of speech and other rights recognised by law that one should consider whether freedom of speech should always be the trump card.

First, some selective comparisons: in England, in terms of the Public Order Act 1986 it is an offence, among other things, for a person to use threatening, abusive or insulting words or behaviour with intent to stir up racial hatred, or if in the circumstances racial hatred is likely to be stirred up. That restriction on freedom of speech is here seen as justifiable because of the harm done to society by that type of speech. In the United States, such a statute could not pass the test of constitutionality. In a well-known case in 1978, a federal court of appeal struck down a local ordinance designed to block a march of American Nazis through a village in which many Jewish survivors of the Holocaust lived. The ordinance was held to be contrary to the First Amendment because it impaired the right of free political expression.[14] In a celebrated judgment in 1919, Justice Oliver Wendell Holmes had said that speech should be punishable only when 'the words used are used in such circumstances and are of such a nature as to create a clear and present danger that they will bring about the substantive evils that Congress has a right to prevent'.[15] This came to be an accepted test, with the result that, however plain the harmful tendencies of a speech or writing, they were immune from legislative control unless the danger to society which they posed was 'clear and present'. Another great American judge, Learned Hand, had suggested an even stricter criterion. Speech, he thought, should not be punishable unless it constituted a direct incitement to violence.[16] In 1969, Judge Learned Hand's test, or something very like it, seems to have been accepted by the Supreme Court, in a case in which a member of the Ku Klux Klan was pros-

[12] *R v Central Independent Television plc* [1994] Fam 192.
[13] Ibid, 203.
[14] *Collin v Smith* 578 F2d 1197 (7th Circuit 1978).
[15] *Schenk v United States* 249 US 47, 51–52 (1919).
[16] *Masses Publishing Co v Patten* 244 Fed 535 (SDNY 1917).

ecuted under an Ohio Act which made it an offence to advocate the necessity of terrorism or illegal action. Going beyond the 'clear and present danger' test, the Court held that under the First Amendment there was a right to advocate the use of force or other unlawful conduct 'except where such advocacy is directed to inciting or producing imminent lawless action and is likely to incite or produce action'.[17] An American writer, one sympathetic to First Amendment rights, has called that case 'the greatest protection to what could be called subversive speech that it has ever had in the United States, and almost certainly greater than such speech has in any other country'.[18]

The Canadian Supreme Court, by contrast, has given more weight to the harm done by what is colloquially called 'hate speech'. It has held that a statute making hate speech criminal was demonstrably justified in a free and democratic society because of the harm which could be expected to result from such speech.[19] Under the European Convention, too, laws prohibiting incitement to racial hatred have been held to be justifiable limitations on the right of free expression.[20] The weight put into the scales is different.

In another recent American case, an Indianapolis ordinance prohibited pornography, which it defined as the 'graphic portrayal of the sexually explicit subordination of women whether in pictures or words'. It was aimed at preventing the display of scenes of degradation, torture and sexual exploitation of women. This was held to be an impermissible limitation on freedom of expression.[21] The ordinance was condemned 'as a form of thought control', which was bad because it restricted that particular form of speech 'no matter how great the artistic, literary or political value of the work as a whole'. The court accepted that the portrayals of women which the ordinance sought to prohibit might well lead to actual harm to women. This was not sufficient to justify it.

This characterisation of the law of the United States is incomplete and somewhat crude. The First Amendment jurisprudence

---

[17] *Brandenburg v Ohio* 395 US 444 (1969).

[18] A Lewis, *Make No Law: The Sullivan Case and the First Amendment* (New York, Random House, 1991) 236. This is a lucid and compulsively readable account of freedom of speech and of the press in the US, and in particular of the litigation culminating in the Supreme Court decision in *New York Times v Sullivan* 376 US 254 (1964).

[19] *R v Keegstra* (1990) 61 CCC (3rd) 1.

[20] *Glimmerveen v The Netherlands* (1979) 4 ECHR 260.

[21] *American Booksellers Association v Hudnut* 111 F2d 323 (1985).

which has flourished since the end of the First World War is complex and sophisticated. It has many nuances. Not all speech is accorded the same value: political speech carries more constitutional weight than commercial speech (that is to say, advertising) or than pornography. There are subtle distinctions drawn in relation to other interests which are to be weighed against freedom of speech. The context of the speech is taken into account. Speech in a military environment is not necessarily as free as it would be in an academic environment. Yet any examination of the recent decisions on the First Amendment plainly shows that it is only the most compelling public interest that may override freedom of speech – and there are very few interests which would be regarded as sufficiently compelling. Although competing public interests are considered, 'ordinarily paramount weight would be given to the public interest in freedom of communication'. This was the conclusion reached by Mason CJ in a recent Australian case upon an analysis of both American and Australian law.[22]

IV. HAS ENGLAND FALLEN BEHIND?

Judged by the measure of the legal protection given to freedom of speech in the United States, England seems to have fallen behind. Although, as Lord Goff said, freedom of speech (as a legal right) has existed in England probably longer than in any other country in the world, we are no longer in the lead. Ought we to be trying to catch up? Many lawyers and many journalists would say so. But before we agree, let us ask two preliminary questions. The first is: why do we recognise the value and importance of freedom of speech? That is not a difficult question to answer on the pragmatic level. Three main objectives have been identified both by judges and by writers on jurisprudence. One of them is that freedom of speech encourages the self-fulfilment of individuals in society. The toleration of a range of ideas, no matter that they are unpopular or even hurtful, fosters the personal development both of those who express the ideas and of those who receive them. A second is that truth is likely to emerge from the free expression of conflicting views. This was the outlook of Justice Holmes (following John Stuart Mill), who saw truth emerging in

---

[22] *Australian Capital Television*, above n 8, 143.

a market place of ideas. In words which still resound after 75 years, he said:[23]

> When men have realised that time has upset many fighting faiths, they may come to believe even more than they believe the very foundations of their own conduct that the ultimate good desired is better reached by free trade in ideas — that the best test of truth is the power of the thought to get itself accepted in the competition of the market.

The third (and to me the most practically important) purpose which freedom of speech is designed to serve is the integrity of democratic government, which requires that opinion and information about those who govern us or who would wish to govern us are available to the electorate. Mason CJ has summed it up by saying that the purpose of protecting the free flow of information, ideas, and debate is to equip the electors to make choices, the elected to make decisions and thereby to enhance the efficacy of representative government.[24]

It is surely material, then, when weighing the right of freedom of speech against other interests, to ask which of the purposes described is served by the freedom claimed. Instead of starting with the assumption that the right to freedom of speech is prima facie entitled to paramount consideration, one may ask, for example, which of the above-mentioned purposes is served by speech which foments racial hatred or which of those purposes is served by pornography depicting the degradation of women. Some would answer that these are not the relevant questions, because any restriction on freedom of speech is the beginning of a slippery slope which must eventually lead to serious erosion of the right. The experience of England does not bear that out. Nor is it in the English legal tradition to decide these questions on the basis of so speculative a generalisation.

Another example: in the United Kingdom there have for many years been statutory limits on the amount of money a parliamentary candidate may spend on his own election. There is a related prohibition of political advertising on radio and television. The object of these laws is to protect the fairness and equality of the political process. The statutes may not entirely achieve these ends, but the desirability of such laws seems to be accepted by all political parties. The US Congress in 1971 passed a law which sought to limit to $50,000 the amount which a candidate

---

[23] *Abrams v United States* 250 US 616, 624 (1919).
[24] *Theophanous*, above n 9, 717.

in a federal election might expend out of his own and his family's monies. It, too, was a measure aimed at preserving the integrity of the political process. The US Supreme Court held, however, that this was an infringement of the First Amendment because it imposed direct restrictions on communication with the electorate and, as the majority put it, restricted the voices of those with money to spend.[25] Marshall J, dissenting,[26] considered that the law was justified to ensure that candidacy did not become the exclusive province of the wealthy, but the majority held this to be an inadequate justification for the interference with the freedom of speech. Similarly, the High Court of Australia has declared invalid an Act of Parliament which prohibited paid advertising on radio or television during an election period on the ground that it infringed the right of communication on matters relevant to political discussion.[27] The majority of the court criticised the law as having the effect of putting opposition parties at a disadvantage, but the basic objection to it was that it restricted free expression of political views by those who might have been able to pay for it. Again, it is useful to ask whether the liberty to spend unrestricted amounts of money on political campaigning and television advertisements assists in the purpose of maintaining effective democratic government.

The second preliminary question one should ask when weighing conflicting interests is whether the interest which comes into conflict with freedom of speech may not itself constitute a fundamental right equally worthy of regard. This question is well illustrated by reference to two branches of the law in which the primacy accorded in the United States to freedom of speech has led to the most radical divergence between that legal system and the English system: contempt of court and defamation.

V. THE LAW OF CONTEMPT OF COURT

The legal tradition in England has been that the right to a fair trial, especially in the criminal courts, is as fundamental and important as the right of free speech. The effect of this recognition has been that comment in relation to a pending trial is restricted by the common law in order to avoid prejudice to the parties to

[25] *Buckley v Valeo* 424 US 1, 17 (1976).
[26] Ibid, 288. See also *First National Bank, Boston v Bellotti* 435 US 765 (1978).
[27] *Australian Capital Television*, above n 8.

litigation and particularly to accused persons. Thus public expressions of opinion on the guilt or innocence of the accused or the publication of facts such as the accused's previous convictions made before or during a trial (or a trial by jury, at least) would be regarded as calculated to prejudice the outcome and to constitute a punishable offence.

A. The *Sunday Times* Case

In *Attorney-General v Times Newspapers*,[28] litigation was pending in the English courts in which damages had been claimed by parents of children affected by the drug thalidomide against the manufacturers of that drug. The case had understandably aroused intense public interest. While negotiations for settlement of the case were in progress, the *Sunday Times* published an article which was found by the House of Lords to have constituted improper pressure on the manufacturers to settle. The case gave the Law Lords the opportunity to deal with the broad issue of pre-trial comment and of contempt of court. Lord Simon of Glaisdale, in his speech, rejected the suggestion that the administration of justice must be paramount in every situation of actual or potential conflict with the right of freedom of discussion:[29]

> Each is a genuine interest of society, and neither can be held to be universally paramount over the other; nor is it really difficult, when the rationale of each is borne in mind, to decide which ought to have paramountcy at any particular moment.

This is the English approach to the weighing of conflicting rights.

As it happened, the *Sunday Times* took the case to the European Commission of Human Rights, which sent it to the European Court of Human Rights. The question before the European Court was whether, under Article 10 of the Convention, the ban on publication while the proceedings were pending was 'necessary in a democratic society . . . for maintaining the authority and impartiality of the judiciary'. By the narrow margin of eleven votes to nine, the Court held that the prohibition or punishment of the publication had not been shown to be necessary for that purpose.[30] In consequence of that judgment, Parliament amended the law

---

[28] [1974] AC 273.
[29] Ibid, 319–20.
[30] *Sunday Times v UK* (1979) 2 EHRR 245.

of contempt of court to give somewhat greater scope for discussion of pending cases.[31] The judgment of the European Court of Human Rights did not meet with universal approval. There was one criticism by an authority always weighty, but who on this occasion might be called unassailable. That critic, of course, was Dr Francis Mann, who commented on the similar decision of the European Commission which had preceded that of the Court. No better tribute can be paid to him than to give this reminder of his incomparable style, particularly when roused. He said that the case involved contempt of court in pending proceedings, 'one of the most exemplary contributions of English law to civilisation, the maintenance of personal liberty and the improvement of standards of public life'.[32] Dr Mann went on:[33]

> Anyone familiar with conditions on the Continent will be conscious of the great evil which trial by newspaper is doing there. It would surely be perplexing if foreign judges who are unaware of the high minded purposes and the lofty rationale of the English rule were to condemn an institution which, however uncertain some of its ramifications may be, is far superior to anything known to their own national legal systems. What matters in the present context is that English courts should appreciate the necessity for adapting their reasoning to the Strasbourg terminology and mentality . . . Sometimes it is not so much the result as the grounds provided for it that would make all the difference for the foreign observer who knows little about the virtues of a legal tradition grown over the centuries and whose instruction in a strange field pre-supposes special sympathy, seeing that he is not always representative of the highest judicial or even legal quality in his own country.

In times when perhaps exaggerated deference is paid to European courts, one misses Francis Mann more than ever. The Strasbourg judgment nonetheless stands, as does the Contempt of Court Act. Neither derogates from the approach to the weighing of rights outlined by Lord Simon in his judgment, a judgment which Dr Mann said 'may seem so persuasive as to be almost inevitable'.[34] The 1981 Act is certainly no open road to the public prejudging of issues in a pending trial.

In the *Sunday Times* case, Lord Reid said that in England there

---

[31] Contempt of Court Act 1981, s 2.
[32] 'Britain's Bill of Rights' (1978) 94 *Law Quarterly Review* 512. This was the text of the 3rd Blackstone Lecture, delivered at the University of Oxford.
[33] Ibid, 529–30.
[34] Ibid, 530.

is a strong feeling that trial by newspaper is wrong and should be prevented:[35]

> What I think is regarded as most objectionable is that a newspaper or television programme should seek to persuade the public, by discussing the issues and evidence in a case before the court, whether civil or criminal, that one side is right and the other side wrong. If we were to ask the ordinary man or even a lawyer in his leisure moments why he has that feeling I suspect that the first reply would be – 'well, look at what happens in some other countries where that is permitted'.

B. The Trial of OJ Simpson and other US Cases

In recent months, we have indeed been looking at what happens in another country, in particular in the State of California. The conduct of the American media in the OJ Simpson trial and of the lawyers outside court has been astonishing to an English lawyer and disquieting to many American lawyers. Leaving aside the televised proceedings – which raises other issues – the particular element causing disquiet is the unrestrained media comment before and during the trial. Views were canvassed on whether the accused was guilty or not – indeed, public opinion polls were taken on the question. During the case, the credibility of the witnesses was daily assessed by 'experts' and evidence or alleged evidence which was not and probably could not have been admitted in court was referred to and discussed. Counsel both for defence and prosecution gave press and television interviews in which they expressed their own confidence in the innocence or guilt of the accused, as the case may be, conduct for which English counsel would be subject to disciplinary proceedings. We should be wrong, however, if we thought that counsel – and, for that matter, the media – behaved as they did simply because they are less moral or professional than we are. That such things could take place is due directly to the relative weight accorded by the American judicial system to the right of free speech as against the right to a fair trial. The virtually unrestrained freedom of comment on a pending trial can be traced to two decisions of the US Supreme Court given in 1941, both, appropriately enough, in appeals from California. In one of them, two union members had been convicted of violence in the course of a labour dispute which had become a

---

[35] [1974] AC 273, 300.

matter of great public interest in California. Before sentence was passed by the judge, the *Los Angeles Times* published a strong editorial. It was headed 'Probation for Gorillas?' The writer said that the judge would be making a serious mistake if he granted probation to the two union members who had been convicted. What was needed, it said, was 'the example of their assignment to the jute mill'. The newspaper was fined for contempt of court.

In the second case, a judge had given a ruling in a dispute between two trade unions. The leader of the union on the losing side sent a telegram to the US Secretary of Labor criticising the judge's decision as outrageous and threatening that enforcement of his order would lead to a strike. He said that the union did not intend to allow a state court to override the majority vote of the members. This, too, was adjudged a contempt of court. When the cases[36] came to the Supreme Court, Justice Frankfurter, dissenting, found in these articles an improper attempt to overawe the judiciary. In his judgment, he freely cited English precedents. But the majority, speaking through Black J, explicitly rejected English practice as a guide. The Court held that the right of free discussion of a matter of general interest overrode any dangers to the judicial process in those two cases. The Court founded its judgment on a broad principle. The First Amendment, it said, required to be given the broadest scope that could be countenanced in an orderly society. Consequently, comment on a pending case should not be punished as contempt unless it raised 'a clear and present danger' of producing unfair administration of justice. It thus applied in this field Justice Holmes's test for political speech. This is a much stricter test, needless to say, than that applied in England. In the OJ Simpson trial it was apparently thought by the judge and the lawyers that any danger to the administration of justice could be averted by sequestering the jury for the duration to keep the media comments from their eyes and ears – with what effects on the jury one can only speculate.

The OJ Simpson case may have been an aberration. In many places in the United States the media observe voluntary codes of restraint. It is nonetheless legitimate to test the American approach by its application to an extreme case. One may ask what purpose that degree of freedom of speech serves in the context of pending trials. It hardly helps in the search for truth. What democratic values does it serve and what would be lost by requiring

[36] *Bridges v California, Los Angeles Times v California* 314 US 252 (1941).

such comments to be reserved until after the case? One may ask why the accused – or, for that matter, the prosecution – should have to submit to every risk of prejudice short of one which would constitute a clear and present danger to the fairness of the trial. In a 1976 decision, the US Supreme Court, through Burger CJ, set aside an order of the Nebraska courts, pending trial of a gruesome murder case, prohibiting the press from reporting a confession made by the defendant to the police as being an improper prior restraint on speech.[37] Such a restraint, he said, was not justifiable unless alternative measures, such as moving the trial to a distant court or delaying it, were shown to be unavailable or ineffectual. Fully accepting the undesirability of prior restraints on the press, we may still wonder that it is the accused who must bear the burden of proving that the alternative measures suggested by the Chief Justice would be ineffectual.

VI. THE LAW OF DEFAMATION

There is another branch of the law in which the weight given to the right of freedom of speech has caused the law of the United States (and also of Australia) to diverge radically from that of England, namely the law of defamation. Any law of libel is a restriction on freedom of speech. Although in England truth is a defence to an action for libel, it has rightly been said that freedom of speech is of limited value if it is no more than freedom to publish the truth. Freedom of speech must at least in some measure include the freedom to err. These are truisms for which no authority need be quoted. Yet the English law of defamation, protective as it is of the reputation of the individual, often penalises even honest error.

The law does not by any means ignore the claims of freedom of speech. A statement otherwise libellous is not actionable if it constitutes comment on a matter of public interest made honestly and without misstatement of fact. The law also realises that in some situations it would not serve the public interest that defamatory allegations could be made only on condition that they could be proved to be true. Those situations, which are fairly clearly

---

[37] *Nebraska Press Association v Stuart* 427 US 539 (1976). Burger CJ was at pains to point out that no right had priority over any other under the Constitution under all circumstances. He nonetheless asserted that freedom of speech from prior restraint 'should have particular force as applied to the reporting of criminal proceedings'.

defined by the common law, give rise to a qualified privilege. In such situations it is enough that the defamatory statements were published in good faith, without malice. Fair and accurate reports of what passes in Parliament and the courts and some other places are also privileged. The categories of qualified privilege, being based on public policy, are not necessarily closed, but the English courts do not readily invent new heads of privilege. This is not, however, a disquisition on the English law of libel. What is important for present purposes is that English law does not recognise any general privilege for the press or for anyone else to defame an individual, even one in a prominent public position, on the grounds that what is said expresses the writer's honest and reasonable belief on a matter which is one of real public interest.[38] This is an undoubted limitation on speech, especially for the press and other media. An editor may have heard a highly discreditable fact about a leading political figure which, if true, the public ought to know. After taking some care to check it, he may firmly believe that it is true. If he publishes it and cannot in the event prove its truth, he will have to pay damages and costs. As juries in England have taken to the habit of awarding enormous damages for libel and as the Court of Appeal regards its power to interfere with those awards as limited,[39] there is peril in attacking the character or conduct of a public man or woman even in good faith. In an appeal to the Privy Council from the West Indies, Lord Bridge said that in a free and democratic society it was almost too obvious to need stating that those who hold office in government must always be open to criticism. 'Any attempt to stifle or fetter such criticism,' he said, 'amounts to political censorship of the most insidious and objectionable kind.'[40] One has seen examples in England (and more so in some foreign countries) of defamation actions being used for just that purpose.[41] In a recent case of the highest importance to freedom of speech in England, the *Derbyshire County Council* case,[42] the House of Lords held

[38] *Campbell v Spottiswoode* (1863) 3 B & S 769, 777; *Blackshaw v Lord* [1984] QB 1.
[39] *Rantzen v Mirror Group Newspapers* (1986) Ltd [1994] QB 670. But see now *John v MGN Ltd, (CA), The Times,* 14 December 1995.
[40] *Hector v Attorney-General of Antigua* [1990] 2 AC 312, 318.
[41] In the Australian High Court Deane J observed that actions for defamation had become a valued source of tax-free profit for holders of public office: *Theophanous,* above n 9, 745.
[42] *Derbyshire County Council v Times Newspapers Ltd* [1993] AC 534.

that a local authority, as an organ of government, could not sue for defamation.[43] In the course of his speech, Lord Keith said:[44]

> What has been described as 'the chilling effect' induced by the threat of civil actions for libel is very important. Quite often the facts which would justify defamatory publication are known to be true, but admissible evidence capable of proving those facts is not available.

It is therefore not surprising that human rights lawyers as well as journalists in England and other countries have looked wistfully at the bold and far-reaching rewriting of the law of defamation by the US Supreme Court some 30 years ago in the great case of *New York Times v Sullivan*.[45]

The circumstances of this case are well known. Let me nonetheless recapitulate its main features. The action arose from an advertisement placed in the *New York Times*, at the height of the American civil rights struggle, by the Committee to Defend Martin Luther King. The advertisement detailed instances of the ferocious suppression of peaceful protest in various towns in the South, and spoke of 'Southern violators of the Constitution'. It specifically referred to the action of the police in Montgomery, Alabama. Sullivan was a Montgomery city commissioner who had the particular duty of supervising the police department of that city. He was not mentioned by name or office, but he nevertheless maintained that the advertisement would be read as referring to him. His action for damages for libel came before an Alabama jury, which awarded him $500,000 in damages, a very considerable sum indeed in 1960. The jury's verdict was welcomed in the South as being a due warning to newspapers like the *New York Times*. It was followed by other writs against the *New York Times*, and against individual journalists and civil rights campaigners, in which huge amounts of damages were claimed. An appeal to the Alabama Supreme Court had been dismissed.

The *New York Times* took its case to the Supreme Court, which reversed the rulings of the Alabama courts in a decision which revolutionised the law of libel as it related to public officials. The main judgment, by Justice Brennan, deserves to be read as law, history, and literature. It is a magnificent judgment by one of

---

[43] Following the judgment of the South African Appellate Division, in which it had been held that the South African Railways (then a department of the government) could not mount an action for defamation: *Die Spoorbond v South African Railways* 1946 AD 999.

[44] [1993] AC 534, 538.

[45] 376 US 254 (1964).

the great judges of our time. It is impossible to read it without a feeling of excitement. It 'strikes the imagination and engages the affections', as the right of property did for Blackstone. In so rich a judgment one can merely outline its result. Founding on the First Amendment, it laid down that when allegations which would ordinarily be defamatory were made of a public official in relation to his official conduct an action by him would not succeed unless he proved that the defamatory statement was false and, what is more, proved with 'convincing clarity' that it was made by the defendant with knowledge of its falsity or with reckless disregard whether it was false or not. Malice in the sense of motive was irrelevant. There was one further important aspect of the judgment. The Alabama courts had held that the criticism of the Montgomery police could be read as a libel on an individual official. Justice Brennan, on the contrary, said that, it being well recognised that no organ of government in the United States could sue for libel, impersonal criticism of government at any level could not be converted 'by some legal alchemy' into libel of the officials of whom the government is composed.[46]

Human rights lawyers, the press, and the broadcasting media look with some longing at this remarkable and resounding vindication of the right of free speech. I hope that I may regard myself as a human rights lawyer, and I have had some experience of acting for the press in defamation actions both in England and in South Africa. Yet I do not share that longing to have the rule in *New York Times v Sullivan* as part of English law.

My reservations are in part practical. The concept of a 'public official' under the *Sullivan* judgment has been extended to public figures generally. It has been held to cover a popular entertainer accused of contacts with the Mafia,[47] and a manager of a football team accused of rigging matches.[48] At least some of the justices of the Supreme Court have suggested that the rule be extended to private persons whose conduct has become a matter of public interest.[49] Moreover, the *Sullivan* decision has not much affected either the prevalence of defamation actions or the generosity of juries. What it has done is to add to the length and cost of libel actions because the plaintiff must be allowed the explore the editorial processes of the defendant newspaper or broadcaster if he is

[46] 376 US 254, 292 (1964).
[47] *Newton v NBC* 930 F2d 662 (1990).
[48] *Curtis Publishing Co v Butts* 388 US 130 (1967).
[49] *Rosenbloom v Metromedia* 403 US 29 (1971).

to have any chance of proving that the latter knew that what he published was untrue. It had been generally recognised that, save in exceptional circumstances, the freedom of the press required that an editor should not be obliged to divulge the sources of his information. In the United Kingdom that protection to the press is embodied in the Contempt of Court Act 1981.[50] In the United States that protection cannot stand against the *Sullivan* rule.

There are more basic reasons for reservations. The most fundamental is that it gives wholly insufficient weight to an individual's right of reputation. A person who goes into public life must expect robust and often unfair criticism. That is part of the price of going into public life. But it does not follow that it is necessary to deprive him or her of any right to reputation. There are surely some libels so gross and offensive that they should be publishable only on condition that they are proved to be true. If it is said of a cabinet minister or a judge that he takes bribes, must he grin and bear it because he cannot prove that the falsehood was a knowing falsehood? The High Court of Australia has been conscious of the unfairness of such a rule. It has in part followed the *Sullivan* judgment, but with the limitation of its scope to persons engaged in politics or government, and with the burden on the defendant of proving that he honestly and reasonably believed in the truth of what he published.[51] This is a fairer rule, but in the case of grossly defamatory allegations of fact it may still be thought to give inadequate protection to the reputation of the plaintiff. Suppose that a newspaper editor is told by a usually reliable informant whom he has no reason to distrust that a cabinet minister has given away state secrets to a foreign power. He believes the story and publishes it. It turns out that it is in fact untrue. Does the public interest in freedom of speech require that it is the innocent plaintiff who should suffer rather than the defendant who erred in his editorial judgment? As the late Lord Goodman said: 'The principle of publish and be damned is a valiant and sensible one for a newspaper. Publish and let someone else be damned is a discreditable principle for a free press.'[52] It was said in the *Sullivan* case that a person in a public position has means at his disposal to answer calumny. Sometimes he has, but often there is no effective answer but legal action. There is a public interest in the good repute of politicians. Are the standards of public life raised by the liberty

---

[50] See s 10; see also *In re an Inquiry* [1988] AC 660.
[51] *Theophanous* and *Stephens*, both above n 9.
[52] Quoted in the Faulks Report on the Law of Defamation (Cmd 5909), 1975.

to savage the reputations of those in public life presently enjoyed by the media in the United States? Well over a hundred years ago, Cockburn CJ said:[53]

> It is said that it is for the interests of society that the public conduct of men should be criticised without any other limit than that the writer should have an honest belief that what he writes is true. But it seems to me that the public have an equal interest in the maintenance of the public character of public men; and public affairs should not be conducted by men of honour . . . if we were to sanction attacks upon them, destructive of their honour and character, and made without any foundation.

We tend to think in terms of an embattled newspaper fighting against the odds to uncover wrongdoing in high places. I knew many editors and journalists in South Africa who ended up not only in the civil courts but in the dock in a criminal court for trying to do just that. But it is not always the case of the courageous editor fighting against the odds. Sometimes it is an embattled plaintiff whom a powerful defendant is trying to discredit and destroy, and whose only redress is an action for defamation. In such a case the *Sullivan* defence does not seem particularly appealing. It is surely not too much to hope that the English law of libel can be reformed without undermining the individual's right to reputation and dignity even if he or she does happen to be in public life. It should not be beyond a court's ability to distinguish in any particular case between hard-hitting political criticism and truly libellous allegations of fact. It is still open to the courts, and if not to the courts to Parliament, to give the presiding judge and the Court of Appeal greater control over awards of damages.[54] The 'chill factor' referred to by Lord Keith in the *Derbyshire County Council* case[55] undoubtedly exists. But it is only one factor. The press in England shows little sign of timidity in its criticism of public figures. Nor have I personally come across a case where an editor who has good reason to believe that there is real political villainy afoot simply lets the story lie on the file.

What are the prospects for the adoption of the *Sullivan* principles or their Australian modification in the English courts? In the *Derbyshire County Council* case in the House of Lords, Lord Keith referred to the *Sullivan* case and said that the public interest

[53] *Campbell v Spottiswoode* (1863) 3 B & S 769, 777.

[54] A recent decision of the Court of Appeal points in that direction, departing in that respect from *Rantzen*, above n 39. See *John v MGN Ltd*, above n 39.

[55] [1993] AC 534, 548.

considerations underlying it were no less valid in England than in the United States.[56] He went no further than that. Indeed, unlike Brennan J, he accepted that if a publication attacking the activities of a governmental authority was also a libel on any individual who managed its affairs that individual himself could bring proceedings for defamation.[57] In the Court of Appeal[58] in that case, two of the Lord Justices referred to *Sullivan* without endorsing its conclusions. The third Lord Justice said expressly that she would not wish to follow *Sullivan* in its refusal of protection to individual politicians.[59] It may be noted that the Supreme Court of Canada has very recently refused to apply either *Sullivan* or its Australian modification.[60] Nor is it clear how any English court, even the House of Lords, could, in the absence of a binding British bill of rights, rewrite English law so as to accord with *Sullivan*.

If an appropriate case arises, the European Court of Human Rights may no doubt be invited to apply the *Sullivan* principles. That Court has not as yet made any move in that direction. Its decisions in freedom of speech cases such as *Lingens v Austria*[61] do not seem to be inconsistent with English law. Whether that Court would in future be receptive to an argument based on *Sullivan* principles I should not like to predict. When Dr Mann wrote the article earlier referred to there were about twenty judges of that Court. There are now over thirty, from very varied legal and political backgrounds.

VII. CONCLUSION

To return to our starting point, at different times different countries have accorded express or implicit primacy to particular rights. Under the German Basic Law, as one might expect given its historical background, the right of individual dignity appears to have pride of place.[62] In the new South African Constitution,

---

[56] Ibid.
[57] Ibid, 550. In South Africa an article criticising the government for racial bias in the exercise of the prerogative of mercy was held to be capable of giving rise to an action for defamation by the (unnamed) minister chiefly responsible for the exercise of the prerogative: *South African Associated Newspapers v Pelser* 1975 (4) SA 797 (AD).
[58] [1992] QB 770.
[59] Ibid, 832 per Butler-Sloss LJ.
[60] *Manning and Church of Scientology of Toronto v Hill* (1995) 126 DLR (4th) 129.
[61] (1986) 8 EHRR 407.
[62] Art 1: 'The dignity of man is inviolable. To respect and protect it shall be the

for obvious reasons, the right of human dignity is also expressly protected;[63] whether it will turn out to be the primary right in South Africa remains to be seen. A judge who has recently been in the Czech Republic tells me that many lawyers in that country regard the right of property as the primary constitutional right. England has no hierarchy of rights. Under the common law there is no reason to fear that freedom of speech will be overborne in importance by any other recognised right. But to take that right to extremes, to attempt to extend its sway over interests hitherto recognised by the common law and by Parliament as equally worthy of protection is likely to damage rather than further the purposes for which it exists. It may indeed reduce rather than increase society's commitment to freedom of speech.

One of the famous aphorisms of Justice Holmes was that the most stringent protection of free speech would not protect a man falsely shouting fire in a crowded theatre.[64] An American wit has said that these days many lawyers think they can win their cases simply by shouting freedom of speech in a crowded court. That was his joke, but it is a joke with a point. Even the best of ideas can be taken too far. More than two hundred years ago, Blackstone said of England that it was 'a land, perhaps the only one in the universe, in which political or civil liberty is the very end and scope of the Constitution'.[65] It is no longer the only one in the universe, but I hope that the rest of the quotation remains true. What we should not assume is that there is only one path to that end, or that we must follow in the footsteps of others to reach it.

POSTSCRIPT

English courts have not adopted the *Sullivan* principle, but there has been a significant development in the law of libel as it affects the press. The House of Lords (with some assistance from New Zealand) has developed a concept of 'responsible journalism' as a defence to libellous allegations in a news report.[66] The success of the defence depends on the degree of public interest, the nature of the allegation and proof of the steps taken to examine its relia-

duty of all public authority.'
[63] The Republic of South Africa Constitution Act, s 10: 'Every person shall have the right to respect for and protection of his or her dignity.'
[64] In *Schenk v United States*, above n 15.
[65] Blackstone, *Commentaries on the Laws of England*, Vol 1, p 6.
[66] *Reynolds v Times Newspapers Ltd* [2001] 2 AC 127.

bility, and, of course, the seriousness of the allegation. In contrast to *Sullivan*, it is not for the plaintiff to prove falsity, and it is for the defendant to prove that its journalism was 'reasonable'.

～

7

A Judge's Duty in a
Revolution – Madzimbamuto
v Lardner-Burke*

~

W
HEN JUDGE NICHOLAS Chambers invited me to
give this year's annual ICLR Lecture, I was told that
the subject of the lecture could be any case reported
in the Law Reports during the past 135 years. I chose *Madzim-bamuto v Lardner-Burke*,[1] an appeal to the Privy Council from
Southern Rhodesia reported in the Appeal Cases of 1969. This once
celebrated constitutional case has passed into history. The case
arose from UDI, the unilateral declaration of independence from
the United Kingdom, made by the Prime Minister of Southern
Rhodesia, Mr Ian Smith, and his Rhodesian Front cabinet. This
declaration was obviously illegal under the existing constitution
of the colony. Nonetheless, the issue of the legality of Mr Smith's
government and its decrees came before the judges of the High
Court of Southern Rhodesia. The litigant who brought the case
before the court was the wife of a black political activist, Mr
Daniel Madzimbamuto who had been detained without trial by
Mr Smith's Minister of Justice, Mr Lardner-Burke. Mrs Madzim-bamuto brought an application for her husband's release on the
grounds that the minister was not in law a minister and had no
legal authority to order the detention. This case was heard by two
courts in Southern Rhodesia and eventually reached the Privy
Council. But Mrs Madzimbamuto's path to the Privy Council was
a long one and entails a quick look at the history of Southern
Rhodesia.

---

* This was the annual lecture of the Incorporated Council of Law Reporting for 2003.
[1] [1969] 1 AC 645.

97

But first, I must answer an obvious question. The colony of Southern Rhodesia became the independent Republic of Zimbabwe in 1980. Mr Smith and his regime disappeared from the political scene. So why choose as the subject of a lecture these old, unhappy, far-off things and battles long ago? There are two reasons. First, the arguments and authorities considered in the three courts covered an unparalleled range of historical and jurisprudential material, including the Statute of Treasons of Henry VII, the writings of Grotius and other seventeenth-century civil lawyers, cases arising after the United States Civil War, the defence of necessity, and the theories of Professor Hans Kelsen, whose concept of the Grundnorm had a rare outing from academia. Second, the case raised in the most direct way the issue of the duty of the Southern Rhodesian judges. These judges, it must be remembered, were the Queen's judges, all of whom had taken an oath of allegiance and a judicial oath. They had sworn to be faithful and bear true allegiance to Her Majesty Queen Elizabeth II, her heirs and successors, according to law, to serve the Queen in the office of judge of the High Court and 'to do right to all manner of people after the laws and usages of Southern Rhodesia . . .'. What were the judges required to do faced with a revolution, albeit a peaceful one, by the government itself? As the independence of the judiciary is a matter of universal concern, the response of the Southern Rhodesian judges to this challenge seems to me a subject of continuing fascination.

There is in fact a third reason why I chose the *Madzimbamuto* case as my subject. I was counsel for Mrs Madzimbamuto in the High Court and the Appellate Division of the High Court of Southern Rhodesia, and then in the Privy Council. Under the current and more relaxed Code of Conduct of the Bar of England and Wales, I believe that sufficient time has passed for me to discuss these cases without impropriety.

Now let me go back to the history. The territory which became Southern Rhodesia and is now Zimbabwe became British by conquest in the late nineteenth century.[2] The territory was formally annexed to the Crown as the colony of Southern Rhodesia in 1923. The ultimate legislative authority therefore remained the United Kingdom Parliament and the Sovereign acting on the advice of her United Kingdom ministers. There was a short period in the late 1950s when the colony became a constituent part of the short-

---

[2] For the early history see *In re Southern Rhodesia* [1919] AC 211.

lived Federation of Rhodesia and Nyasaland. On the dissolution of the Federation, the Parliament of the United Kingdom passed an Act[3] which authorised the Queen by Order in Council to grant to Southern Rhodesia a new constitution, providing for a greater degree of self-government. Under this constitution, known as the 1961 Constitution, the Queen was represented by a Governor who was to act on the advice of a cabinet of Southern Rhodesian ministers, who were responsible to the elected legislature of the colony. The significant change was that the Southern Rhodesian legislature could, subject to a few exceptions, by a special procedure amend the constitution itself. The exceptions included the position of Her Majesty as Sovereign, the appointment of the Governor, appeals to the Privy Council (which were preserved), and the composition of the legislature. Under the 1961 Constitution, Southern Rhodesia remained a Crown Colony over which the United Kingdom Parliament retained complete legislative power. Southern Rhodesia was therefore something of a hybrid. It was not a self-governing dominion but it had more self-government than most Crown Colonies.[4]

At the root of Mr Smith's declaration of independence was the Southern Rhodesian franchise. The existing franchise qualifications were not expressed in racial terms. They were expressed in terms of property ownership, income and level of education, but, given the poverty of the African population and their lower level of education, the franchise was in practice heavily weighted in favour of the white population. The white population in 1965 was no more than 220,000; the black population was over 4 million. Yet in 1965 the legislative assembly had fifty-one white members (all but one belonging to Mr Smith's Rhodesian Front) and thirteen African members. Under the 1961 Constitution, special procedures were required for altering the qualifications of voters. Even under the 1961 Constitution it would have been many years before black voters acquired parity with white voters, let alone majority rule, but the policy of the United Kingdom, whether under Labour or Conservatives, was movement towards parity and, at some undefined future time, majority rule. Mr Smith's frankly avowed policy was 'no majority rule in my lifetime'. (Mr Smith is still alive.) The maintenance of white political supremacy was the admitted

[3] The Southern Rhodesian (Constitution) Act 1961.

[4] The constitutional and political history of the colony before UDI is fully covered by C Palley, *The Constitutional History and Law of Southern Rhodesia, 1888–1965* (Oxford, Oxford University Press, 1966).

motive for Mr Smith's attempt to escape the sovereignty of the United Kingdom.

I shall not recount the events of the period before the Unilateral Declaration of Independence on 11 November 1965. I would note only that on 6 November the Southern Rhodesian government lawfully declared a state of emergency. On that day, acting under emergency powers, Mr Lardner-Burke as Minister of Justice issued a detention order against Mr Daniel Madzimbamuto. It was at no time disputed that Mr Madzimbamuto's detention at that stage was lawful.

On 11 November Mr Smith and his cabinet proclaimed their Declaration of Independence. They prefaced their Declaration with a lame, and indeed impertinent, parody of the American Declaration of Independence.[5] In this Declaration, Mr Smith purported to declare the country an independent sovereign state and to 'give' to the country a new constitution in place of the 1961 Constitution. Under this constitution, throughout referred to as the 1965 Constitution, the title of Queen of Rhodesia was conferred on Her Majesty Queen Elizabeth II,[6] and the functions of the governor would be vested in 'the officer administering the government'. Under the 1965 Constitution the existing legislative assembly was to continue, but as the Parliament of Rhodesia; and the existing cabinet continued in office.

The United Kingdom government (then Mr Harold Wilson's government) reacted immediately. Her Majesty, acting in terms of her powers under the 1961 Constitution, dismissed what had been Her Majesty's ministry in Southern Rhodesia. A few days later the United Kingdom Parliament passed the Southern Rhodesia Act 1965, which declared that Southern Rhodesia continued to be part of Her Majesty's dominions, and authorised Her Majesty by Order-in-Council to make laws for Southern Rhodesia.

In pursuance of that power, Her Majesty made an order[7] declaring 'for the avoidance of doubt' that the purported promulgation of the 1965 Constitution was void and of no effect, and that henceforth no laws might be made by the legislature of Southern Rhodesia. There was no doubt that, under the constitutional provisions governing Southern Rhodesia at the time of the Declaration

---

[5] Two aspects of the American declaration were omitted from Mr Smith's proclamation. He forbore to assert that 'all men are created equal' and that the governmental power was derived 'from the consent of the governed'.

[6] Needless to say, a title never accepted by Her Majesty.

[7] The Southern Rhodesian (Constitution) Order 1965 (SI 1965/1952).

of Independence, the United Kingdom Act of Parliament and the Queen's Order-in-Council had the force of law.

Mr Smith paid no heed to them. The legislature, acting as the Parliament of Rhodesia under the 1965 Constitution, continued to pass laws, and the ministers continued to exercise executive powers. The civil service continued to obey the directions of Mr Smith's government, as did the police and the army. The fact was that Mr Smith's legislature and executive had effective control of the whole country.

On the other hand, the United Kingdom government had declared its intention to restore constitutional government to Southern Rhodesia. Mr Wilson had at an early stage disavowed the use of force but applied economic sanctions, which were in due course strengthened by a resolution of the United Nations. No foreign government, not even South Africa, accorded de jure or de facto recognition to the new regime.

Although, under the United Kingdom Act of Parliament, the Queen had full power to make laws for Southern Rhodesia, she in fact did not make any laws. The Governor remained in his official residence in Salisbury, as it then was, and did not resign his office as Governor under the 1961 Constitution, but with trivial exceptions did not exercise any of his functions under that Constitution. Immediately after UDI he received instructions from the Queen which he passed on to the citizens of the colony. This was the Governor's statement:

> In accordance with the Queen's instructions I have informed Mr Smith and his colleagues that they no longer hold office. I call on the citizens of Rhodesia to refrain from all acts which would further the objects of the illegal authorities. Subject to that, it is the duty of all citizens to maintain law and order in this country and to carry on with their normal tasks. This applies equally to the judiciary, the armed services, the police and the public service.

This message became the subject of considerable debate in the courts.[8]

I must now go back to Mr Madzimbamuto. Under what I will call the 1961 laws, the state of emergency proclaimed by the Governor on 6 November 1965 automatically expired after three months. Immediately before its expiry, the Parliament sitting under the 1965 Constitution authorised the extension of the state of emergency and authorised regulations providing for the continued

[8] For the full text see [1969] 1 AC 645, 714–15.

detention of any person detained under the preceding emergency. Mr Madzimbamuto thus remained in prison. It was at that stage that Mrs Madzimbamuto applied to the High Court for the release of her husband and a declaration that his continued detention was illegal. At the end of June 1966 her case came before two judges of the High Court. Mrs Madzimbamuto's case was fundamentally a simple one. Under the Roman-Dutch law, which was the common law of Southern Rhodesia, as under English law, every interference with liberty is prima facie unlawful and must be justified. She submitted that, under the 1961 Constitution and in light of the United Kingdom legislation which had followed the Declaration of Independence, no decrees or actions purportedly taken under the authority of the 1965 Constitution had any legal validity. Her husband's detention could therefore not be legally justified.[9]

I have not so far said anything about the position of the High Court under the 1965 Constitution. At the time of the Unilateral Declaration of Independence, all the judges of the High Court had taken the oaths to which I have referred. The 1965 Constitution provided that every judge appointed under the 1961 Constitution could continue in office as if he had been appointed under the 1965 Constitution. But the 1965 Constitution also provided that the Prime Minister could require a judge 'to state forthwith whether he accepts this Constitution'. If the judge refused to do so, his office would be deemed to have become vacant. None of the judges had been called upon by the Prime Minister to state whether they accepted the 1965 Constitution and none of them had done so. The two judges hearing the case sat as judges under the 1961 Constitution and made it clear throughout that they were doing so.

The Smith government did not ignore these court proceedings. From the beginning, it treated the case as a test of its authority. Mr Lardner-Burke, who was Mr Smith's Minister of Justice and who was the first respondent in the case, boldly contended that, as there had been a successful revolution, the old 1961 order had been completely replaced by a new, 1965, order. Whether the new order had come about in a legitimate way or not was irrelevant. Thus, strangely enough, the Smith government in those proceedings recognised that the judges were sitting as judges under the

---

[9] Mr Leo Baron, an attorney who had also been detained on the order of Mr Lardner-Burke, made a similar application. His case and Mrs Madzimbamuto's were heard together in both the Southern Rhodesian courts.

1961 Constitution and had not accepted the 1965 Constitution, yet it was asking those judges to declare that the 1961 Constitution had disappeared and been replaced by a new one.

When I was a law student a good deal of time was devoted in the jurisprudence course to the writings of Professor Hans Kelsen. One would hardly have guessed that Professor Kelsen would be extensively quoted and relied on in British colonial courts in the years to come.[10] Professor Kelsen's doctrine was that all the norms or rules of a legal order derive their ultimate validity from a basic law or grundnorm, usually a constitution. When we reach that ultimate constitution, we cannot look beyond it: we must simply presuppose its validity. If that ultimate basic law is displaced, for example by a revolution, and the citizens of the state accept the new order, that new order becomes the grundnorm from which all legal authority will in future be derived. Counsel for Mr Lardner-Burke submitted that that is what had happened in Southern Rhodesia. He was able to refer to judgments of the Supreme Courts of Pakistan[11] and Uganda,[12] which, sitting after coups d'état, had on the basis of Kelsen's theory held that the old constitution had been effectively annulled and that there was a new grundnorm in each of those countries.

This argument did not convince the High Court. It held that, even if the Smith government was at present in complete and effective control of Rhodesia, it could not be said that there had been a successful revolution. The United Kingdom had not abandoned sovereignty over the country, nor could it be said that the measures taken by the British Government to put an end to the revolution would be doomed to failure. Lewis J, the presiding judge, emphasised that the judges derived their powers from the 1961 Constitution. He said that, if he were to hold that the 1965 Constitution was the legal constitution of the country and the rebel government was the lawful government, he would be false to his judicial oath and false to his own oath of allegiance. He said that any judge who took up office under the 1965 Constitution would be taking up such office purely through political expediency,[13] would be aiding the government from a political

---

[10] In particular, his *General Theory of Law and the State* (Cambridge, MA, Harvard University Press, 1945).

[11] *The State v Dosso* [195S] 2 PSCR 180.

[12] *Uganda v Commissioner of Prisons, Ex p Matovu* [1966] EA 514.

[13] He pointed out that anyone who took office as a judge under the 1965 Constitution would have to take an oath of allegiance to 'the Queen of Rhodesia', whereas no person held such a title.

point of view, that his decisions upholding everything done under the 1965 Constitution would have no value as legal decisions, and could not confer de jure status on the government in either internal or international law.

But Mr Lardner-Burke had an alternative argument. He argued that, even if Mr Smith's government was not the de jure government, it was the de facto government in that it was the only effective government of the country. The court should therefore recognise at least those of its acts which were done for the preservation of law and order.

The concepts of de jure and de facto governments are well known in international law and relate to the recognition by foreign governments of a new government or regime in an existing state. Here the court was asked to apply the concept of de facto recognition to an illegal government sitting within the territory of the court's own jurisdiction.

On the other side, the argument for Mrs Madzimbamuto was unequivocal. The fact that the present government was in effective control of the country was irrelevant. The court, being bound by the 1961 Constitution, could not recognise the so-called Parliament of Rhodesia; nor could it recognise any actions of ministers who had been dismissed by the Queen. The court should not be swayed by arguments that the measures of the unlawful regime were necessary for the preservation of peace and good government. The way to preserve those was for the rebel regime to return to legality.

The court described this as a very far-reaching submission – as, indeed, it was. What it meant, they said, was that since 11 November 1965 there had been a vacuum in the law of Southern Rhodesia.

Lewis J and his colleague (Goldin J) held that it was not for the court to try to force the government to abandon the revolution, even supposing that it could do so. They were prepared to recognise the admittedly illegal regime as a de facto government. They took comfort from two remarkable sources of authority. The first was a passage in the celebrated work of the great seventeenth-century Dutch jurist Grotius, *De Jure Belli ac Pacis* [The Law of War and Peace]. This classic work laid the foundations of modern international law. Grotius was also, of course, one of the greatest writers on the classical Roman-Dutch law which was the common law both of South Arica and of Southern Rhodesia. The passage on which the judges relied fell under the subtitle

'How far obedience should be rendered to a usurper of sovereign power'. In this passage, Grotius speaks of the usurper who has unlawfully assumed power in a state:

> 1. . . . Now while such usurper is in possession the acts of government which he performs may have a binding force, arising not from a right possessed by him, for no such right exists, but from the fact that the one to whom the sovereignty actually belongs, whether people, or king, or senate, would prefer that measures promulgated by him should meanwhile have the force of law, in order to avoid the utter confusion that would result from the subversion of laws and suppression of the courts.

However,

> 2. In the case of measures promulgated by the usurper . . . which have as their purpose to establish him in his unlawful possession, obedience is not to be rendered unless disobedience would involve grave danger.[14]

It is easy to see why counsel for Mr Lardner-Burke relied strongly on this statement by one of the greatest of European lawyers. There was in it an echo of that part of the Governor's message where, in the name of the Queen, he stated that 'it is the duty of all citizens to maintain law and order in the country and to carry on with their normal tasks'.

The second source of authority relied on by the judges was a series of cases in the United States Supreme Court. At the end of the American Civil War questions arose in the United States courts whether any recognition should be given to any official acts of the Confederate States performed while those states were in rebellion against the United States. So one had the extraordinary sight of counsel and judges in wigs and gowns in the heat of tropical Africa debating in detail judgments which in their own country had passed into legal history.

The cases were undoubtedly fascinating in themselves. The leading case was *Texas v White*.[15] There, Chase CJ held in the first place that the Confederacy itself and its constitution were 'absolutely null' and that the legislature of Texas, established in hostility to the constitution of the United States, could not be regarded in the courts of the United States as a lawful legislature

---

[14] *De Jure Belli ac Pacis* I.4.XV, trans FW Kellsley (Oxford, Oxford Universioty Press, 1925). Counsel for Mr Lardner Burke also referred to such civilian authors as Vitoria, Suarez, Cocceius and Pufendorf.
[15] 7 Wallace 700 (1868).

or its acts as lawful acts. Nonetheless, the government of Texas during the secession was in full control of that state as a de facto government. Then he said, in words constantly quoted in later cases and adopted by the Southern Rhodesian court:[16]

> Acts necessary to peace and good order among citizens, such, for example, as acts sanctioning and protecting marriage and domestic relations regulating the conveyance and transfer of property . . . and providing remedies for injuries and other similar acts which would be valid if emanating from a lawful government must be regarded, in general as valid when proceeding from an actual though unlawful government.

Later cases extended the scope of acts which could be recognised to police regulations and the prosecution of crimes. But every American judgment excluded from recognition any acts which tended to impair the supremacy of the national authority (ie the United States) or which impaired the rights of citizens under the United States Constitution.[17]

On these precedents, the High Court, sitting as a court under the 1961 Constitution, held that the declaration of the state of emergency and the detention of Mr Madzimbamuto, although unlawful, should be recognised as valid measures taken for the maintenance of peace and order by a de facto government. Lewis J summed up his conclusions by saying:[18]

> On the basis of necessity and in order to avoid chaos and a vacuum in the law, the court would give effect to such measures of the effective government as could lawfully have been taken by the lawful government under the 1961 Constitution for the preservation of peace and good government and the maintenance of law and order. The extensions of the state of emergency and the detention measures were all within that category; they had not been shown in their purpose to have been hostile to the authority of the sovereign power or to have impaired the just rights of citizens under the 1961 Constitution or to have been taken with actual intent to further the revolution.

Goldin J reached a similar conclusion. So Mrs Madzimbamuto's application was dismissed.

---

[16] Ibid, 733.

[17] Among the many cases cited were *Horn v Lockhart* 17 Wallace 570 (1873), *US v Insurance Companies* 22 Wallace 99 (1874) and *Baldy v Hunter* 171 US 388 (1898).

[18] The case in the High Court is reported in the South African Law Reports 1966 (2) SA 445. The judgments were subjected to critical analysis by RS Welsh, 'The Constitutional Case in Southern Rhodesia' (1967) 83 *Law Quarterly Review* 64 and AJE Jaffey, 'The Rhodesian Constitutional Cases' (1968) 8 *Rhodesian Law Journal* 138.

One can well understand and even sympathise with the unusual position in which the judges found themselves. Nonetheless, their judgments gave rise to some troubling questions.

First, the recognition of the regime as a de facto government. Such recognition by the sovereign's own court was not only unprecedented but contradictory. The judges adopted, from an English case, the definition of a de facto government as one exercising all the functions of government, including maintaining courts of justice.[19] When a government does not appoint its own judges but submits the question of its status to the courts of the lawful sovereign, how then can it be a de facto government? As to Grotius, should he not be read as giving sensible advice to subjects in the power of the usurper rather than legal advice to the sovereign's judges? In *Texas v White* and the other United States cases, the acts recognised as valid after the Civil War were acts related to property, contracts, marriages, and ordinary crimes. Save for arrests on ordinary criminal charges, there is no case in which the executive's interference with the liberty of the subject was recognised.[20] Moreover, the courts would not recognise any act done in conflict with the Constitution of the United States or which impaired the supremacy of the lawful government. One recalls that the Governor's message called upon all citizens 'to refrain from all acts which might further the objectives of the illegal authorities'. Surely there was no act more likely to further the objectives of the illegal authorities and to impair the supremacy of the lawful government than the act of the court itself in recognising the rebel regime as a de facto government? Nor could there surely be anything more calculated, in Grotius's phrase, to establish the usurper in his unlawful possession.

That was certainly the view of Mr Smith himself. In a speech made on the day that the judgment was given, Mr Smith declared the judgment to be a victory as it accorded his government 'de facto recognition'. What the effect would have been if the court had refused recognition one can only speculate. There was certainly

[19] *The Arantzazu Mendi* [1939] AC 256, 264 per Lord Atkin.

[20] These US cases were referred to by Lord Wilberforce in the House of Lords in relation to the question whether UK courts could give recognition to any measure of a government not recognised by the UK. He regarded these cases as showing 'that where private rights, or acts of everyday occurrence, or perfunctory acts of administration are concerned (the scope of these exceptions has never been precisely defined) the courts may, in the interests of justice and common sense, where no consideration of public policy to the contrary has to prevail, give recognition to the actual facts or realities found to exist in the territory in question': *Carl Zeiss Stiftung v Rayner & Keeler Ltd (No 2)* [1967] 1 AC 853, 954.

one aspect of executive power which the Smith government did not venture to exercise as long as its legal status remained doubtful. At this time there were many prisoners under sentence of death, their appeals exhausted, who had been awaiting execution for months, even years. Those who had the task of hanging the condemned men apparently had qualms about doing so on the orders of an unlawful government.

Nor do the judgments seem to have paid much attention to the rights of Mr Madzimbamuto himself. He was detained, as the court itself found, by an unlawful government on the orders of persons holding no office under the 1961 Constitution. What of his constitutional right to liberty? The judges had sworn to 'do right to all manner of people after the laws and usages of Southern Rhodesia'. Under those laws and usages his detention was plainly illegal. Some might say that the duty of the court was to do right to Mr Madzimbamuto, not to fill a supposed vacuum in the law. The High Court gave its judgment in September 1966. Mrs Madzimbamuto appealed to the Appellate Division of the High Court, where a hearing before five judges began on 30 January 1967. The Appellate Division was presided over by the Chief Justice, Sir Hugh Beadle, a considerable figure in Southern Rhodesian political and legal history. It must be emphasised that neither the Chief Justice nor his colleagues at that stage had joined the revolution. No member of the court had taken the oath under the 1965 Constitution. Consequently, when the appeal hearing began the judges were still sitting as judges under the 1961 Constitution. Indeed, at the beginning of the appeal the Smith government did not persist in its contention that the 1965 Constitution was a lawful constitution.

After lengthy argument, judgment was reserved. Some months later, and before judgment was given, the court asked for further argument on a number of points. The main question raised by the court was whether the citizens of Southern Rhodesia (presumably including the judges) still owed allegiance to Her Majesty. They also wished to hear argument on whether the English Statute of Treason of 1495 (11 Hen 7, c 1) applied to the situation in Southern Rhodesia. In addition, notwithstanding the original disavowal by counsel for the government, the court invited argument on whether the 1965 Constitution had become the lawful constitution of Southern Rhodesia. I should immediately say, for the benefit of those not familiar with the Treason Act of 1495, that that statute was a product of the Wars of the Roses, during which the possession of the English throne had fluctuated with the fortunes of war. What it provided, in brief, was that allegiance was owed by subjects to the king 'for the time being', and that those who served him would not be liable to be convicted of high treason if the rightful king regained the throne. The king for the time being might be called a de facto king. These points were enthusiastically taken up by counsel for the Smith government. The hearing resumed in October 1967 and judgment was given on 29 January 1968, a full year after the appeal had begun.

The five judgments of the appellate judges take up 197 printed pages.[21] I shall not attempt to do more than give the gist of them. The Chief Justice held that, although the court had originated from the 1961 Constitution, that constitution was 'in suspension' and likely to remain so, and therefore the court did not derive its present authority from that source. On the other hand, he said, the court did not derive its authority from the 1965 Constitution, which was not the de jure constitution. The court derived its authority simply from the fact that the government in power allowed it to function. The regime was a fully de facto government and could lawfully do anything which its predecessors could lawfully have done under the 1961 Constitution. On this basis, the emergency measures of the government were to be regarded as lawful. Sir Hugh said it was an admittedly unprecedented solution to an unprecedented problem. In the course of argument, he suggested an analogy. He said that, by the year 1900, zoologists believed that they knew of the existence of every possible genus of large animal. But then an explorer in central Africa discovered the okapi. Although the okapi could not be fitted in to any known genus, that did not justify a refusal to acknowledge the animal's existence. Perhaps, he said, the case before him might be the okapi of jurisprudence. Counsel respectfully responded that at least the okapi was discovered and not invented.

Jarvis J, on the other hand, stated that the court remained a court under the 1961 Constitution, as the regime had not usurped the functions of that court. The regime was not the lawful government but did constitute a de facto government. Like the High Court, he was prepared to give legal effect to its declaration of emergency and its detention measures.

Macdonald J took a radically different approach. He held that

---

[21] The judgments are reported 1968 (2) SA 284. These judgments too have been critically analysed, by Jaffey, above n 3, and by RS Welsh (1970) 87 *South African Law Journal* 168.

allegiance was now owed exclusively to 'the State of Rhodesia', as the Queen through her United Kingdom Government had withdrawn its protection from Southern Rhodesia and thus forfeited her claim to its allegiance. The government was a de jure government and the 1965 constitution was the de jure constitution, and the court was exercising its power under the authority of the new regime and not under the 1961 Constitution.

Quenet J also held that the 1961 Constitution had disappeared. The regime and the 1965 Constitution had acquired what he called 'internal de jure status'. Thus two of the judges had asserted that the 1965 Constitution was now the legal constitution under which they exercised their authority, while a third, Beadle CJ, while not going so far, had held that the 1961 Constitution was no longer operative.

The fifth judgment was given by Fieldsend J. I venture the respectful opinion that Fieldsend J's judgment is the clearest and above all the most principled of the seven judgments given by the Rhodesian courts in the Madzimbamuto case. Fieldsend J held that the Southern Rhodesian courts derived their existence and powers solely from the 1961 Constitution, and that in ruling upon the validity of any legislation their yardstick must be the 1961 Constitution.[22] As to the approach of the Chief Justice, the fact that the rebel regime had allowed the court to sit could not constitute a new basis for its jurisdiction. The judicial power was still exercised in the name of the lawful sovereign, and the rebel regime, not having a judicial arm, could not be said to be a de facto government. In any event, a court owing its existence to a lawful constitutional order could not recognise the existence within its own jurisdiction of a rebel de facto government. Fieldsend J said:

> Judges appointed to office under a written constitution, which provides certain fundamental laws and restricts the manner in which those laws can be altered, must not allow rights under that constitution to be violated. This is a lasting duty for so long as they hold office, whether the violation be by peaceful or revolutionary

---

[22] He pertinently quoted a passage from the judgment of Taney CJ in the US Supreme Court in a case arising from an internal rebellion in the state of Rhode Island in the 1840s: 'And if a State court should enter upon the inquiry proposed in this case, and should come to the conclusion that the government under which it acted had been put aside, it would cease to be a court and be incapable of pronouncing a judicial decision upon the question which it undertook to try. If it decides at all as a court, it necessarily affirms the existence and authority of the government under which it is exercising judicial power.' *Luther v Borden* 7 Howard 1, 39–40 (1849).

means. . . . The court must stand in the way of a blatantly illegal
attempt to tear up a constitution. If to do this is to be characterised
as counter-revolutionary, surely an acquiescence in illegality must
equally be revolutionary. Nothing can encourage instability more
than for any revolutionary movement to know that if it succeeds in
snatching power it will be entitled ipso facto to the complete support
of the pre-existing judiciary in their judicial capacity. It may be a
vain hope that the judgment of a court will deter a usurper, or have
the effect of restoring legality, but for a court to be deterred by fear
of failure is merely to acquiesce in illegality.

Fieldsend J nonetheless held that, although the rebel government
could not be recognised as even a de facto government, the neces-
sities of the factual situation might require the court to recognise
some particular acts directed to and reasonably required for the
ordinary running of the state. On the evidence of the security
situation in Southern Rhodesia, he was prepared to find that the
continuance of a state of emergency was necessary for the preservation of peace and order.

As it happens, the judges in the Appellate Division had discerned
a flaw in the regulation under which Mr Madzimbamuto was
being held, a flaw which had nothing to do with the constitutional
question. On that ground alone they upheld the appeal knowing
that the government could (as it did) correct the flaw within
twenty-four hours. Their judgments on the constitutional issue
stood notwithstanding Mrs Madzimbamuto's technical victory,
and Mr Madzimbamuto remained in prison.

Mrs Madzimbamuto did not accept that this was the end of the
line. She applied to the Appellate Division for leave to appeal
to the Privy Council. At the same time, a similar application
was made on behalf of three condemned Africans whose attempt
to prevent their execution by the Smith government had been
rejected by the Appellate Division. Their application and Mrs
Madzimbamuto's were both refused. It was open, however, to Mrs
Madzimbamuto to approach the Privy Council itself for leave to
appeal. The three Africans were theoretically also entitled to make
an application to the Privy Council, but at that stage the Solicitor
General, speaking on behalf of the Smith government, informed
the Court that no order of the Privy Council would be obeyed in
Rhodesia and, if the Appellate Division were to order a stay of
the execution pending an appeal to the Privy Council, that order
would likewise be disobeyed. The Solicitor General's statement,
a defiance of the Court, and its acceptance without demur by

Sir Hugh Beadle and the other members of Court[23] led to the resignation of Fieldsend J. Within the week, the regime, its legal authority now endorsed by a majority of the Appellate Division, exercised that authority, not uncharacteristically, by hanging the three Africans. Thereafter the remainder of the Rhodesian judiciary, with one exception, continued in office, recognising the 1965 Constitution.

Mrs Madzimbamuto got to the Privy Council. Her application for leave to appeal against the Rhodesian judgment was accepted, notwithstanding the Smith government's statement that it would not obey an order of the Privy Council.[24]

In the Privy Council I again appeared for Mrs Madzimbamuto, together with Mr Louis Blom-Cooper, whose knowledge of British colonial law was unrivalled. Needless to say, the Rhodesian ministers took no part in the proceedings, but Mr Godfray Le Quesne QC appeared as amicus curiae. Over nine days in the Privy Council all the precedents were again debated at length – Kelsen, Grotius, the American cases, the Treason Act 1495. Some five weeks later the Privy Council upheld the appeal. The judgment of the majority of their Lordships was delivered by Lord Reid. Their conclusion was that the acts of the UDI Parliament and Ministry were without any legal validity. Lord Reid stated that the Queen in the Parliament of the United Kingdom remained Sovereign in Southern Rhodesia. As to de facto and de jure governments, those were concepts of international law, quite inappropriate in dealing with the legal position of a usurper within a territory in which the Sovereign's judges still sat. Both the judges in the High Court and three in the Appellate Division had disavowed any suggestion that they were sitting as a court under the revolutionary constitution of 1965. The Statute of Treason of 1495, said Lord Reid, did no more than excuse a subject's obedience to a king de facto. It did not require recognition by the judges of the acts of a usurping government. The American cases were carefully examined. Lord Reid's conclusion was that they were concerned only with the civil claims of individuals after the end of the Civil War. None of them were cases of courts called upon during the rebellion to pass upon the legality of the governments of the rebel states or the validity of their legislation. None of the cases conferred validity upon acts of the Confederate States which were contrary

---

[23] See *Dhlarmni v Carter* 1968 (2) SA 44.
[24] See [1969] 1 AC 645, 661.

to the United States Constitution. As to Grotius, it may be that he had stated a general principle, and had recognised the need to preserve law and order in territory controlled by a usurper, but no such principle could override an act of the Parliament of the United Kingdom. Lord Reid acknowledged that Her Majesty's judges in Southern Rhodesia had been put in an extremely difficult position. But, he said, the fact that the judges had been put in this position could not justify disregard of the legislation passed or authorised by the United Kingdom Parliament. The Queen's Order-in-Council of 1965 had declared that every act done under the purported 1965 Constitution was void and of no effect; no doctrine of necessity could override that law of the Sovereign power. Lord Reid's judgment was concurred in by Lord Morris of Borth-y-Gest, Lord Wilberforce, and Lord Pearson. Lord Pearce dissented. He held that there was scope, albeit limited, for the operation of the doctrine of necessity as defined in the judgment of Fieldsend J.

The Rhodesian judges did not accept the decision of the Privy Council. They continued to sit, but now as judges under the 1965 Constitution. Apart from Fieldsend J, the only exception was Dendy Young J. The refusal of his colleagues to recognise the Privy Council judgment prompted his resignation.

So ended the case of *Madzimbamuto v Lardner-Burke*. There had been seven judgments in Rhodesia and two in London. I respectfully suggest that the majority in the Privy Council gave the right judgment. But my theme is not so much the merits of the judgments as the conduct of the judges. Faced with the revolution, did they do their judicial duty? Their duty as judges, in the case of all of them, stemmed from their acceptance of the Queen's Commission and their oaths. Their oath of allegiance to the Queen was an oath of allegiance to the lawful 1961 Constitution. Their second oath was to do right to all manner of people after the laws and usages of Southern Rhodesia. At the time of UDI there was no doubt what the laws and usages of Southern Rhodesia were. They included the 1961 Constitution and the constitutional sovereignty of the Queen and the United Kingdom Parliament. It was clear what was lawful and what was not. Lewis J and Goldin J had both said that it was not the function of a court to attempt to end the revolution and restore legality. Beadle CJ endorsed that view. That was tantamount to saying that the court must not choose between legality and illegality. But, as Fieldsend J had said in the passage I have already quoted, if a court standing in the way of a blatantly illegal attempt to tear up a constitution is to be characterised as counter-revolutionary, surely an acquiescence in illegality must equally be revolutionary? Until three judges of the Appellate Division had said that the 1961 Constitution was at an end the Smith government had not indicated that it would disobey the decisions of the court. There was, no doubt, a real possibility that if the judges had refused to give any recognition to the acts of the unlawful government they would have been removed and replaced with more amenable judges. But that would not have been an easy political decision for Mr Smith. And if adherence to legality had led to their forcible removal, that would have been one of those consequences which, on high authority, judges ought to disregard.

In 1879 the government of what was then the Cape Colony, acting without lawful authority, arrested a local chieftain and in justification contended that the disturbed state of the country necessitated the arrest. One of the greatest of South African judges, de Villiers CJ (later Lord de Villiers), said, however:

> The disturbed state of the country ought not . . . to influence the Court for its first and most sacred duty is to administer justice and not to preserve the peace of the country . . . the civil courts have but one duty to perform and that is to administer the laws of the country without fear, favour or prejudice independently of the consequences which ensue.[25]

Eighty years later, in an English case arising from Northern Rhodesia (as it then was), an English judge said

> There may come times in a country's history when it may appear highly inconvenient or politically hazardous that the law should pursue its course, but in a court of law such considerations are irrelevant and cannot serve to deprive the subject of a right . . .[26]

The High Court judges and Sir Hugh Beadle responded by saying that circumstances were different or, as I would put it, that that great principle applies only when it does not really matter.

I have no doubt that until the end of the *Madzimbamuto* case it was entirely right for the judges to remain in office, in accordance with the Governor's direction. But, once Mr Smith had made it clear after the Appellate Division had given judgment that his government would not accept any limitation of its powers and

---

[25] *In re Willem Kok* 1879 9 Buchanan 45, 66.
[26] *Ex p Mwenya* [1960] 1 QB 241, 308 per Sellers LJ.

would disobey orders of court not consonant with the 1965 Constitution, I find it difficult to see how the judges could continue in office consistently with their oaths. As a matter of personal and political decision, it was open to any of the judges to resign the Queen's Commission, to adhere to the revolution and to take office under the 1965 Constitution. But none of them was prepared to do that. Those who continued to sit and to apply the 1965 Constitution purported to do so by reason of purely legal considerations. Some spoke of their duty to continue to administer justice, and of the 'chaos' which would ensue if the Privy Council judgment was to be accepted. There was no mention of the terms of the oaths[27] under which they had taken office, nor of their duty to protect citizens from unlawful executive action.

Lord Atkin once said in a case which reached the Privy Council from Nigeria that on issues affecting the liberty of the British subject 'it is the tradition of British justice that judges should not shrink from deciding such issues in the face of the executive'.[28]

Did the majority of the Rhodesian judges act in that tradition? I fear that they did not.

In my respectful opinion, the honour of the Southern Rhodesian judiciary was maintained by Dendy Young and Fieldsend JJ. In his letter to the Governor seeking to be released from his judicial duties, Fieldsend J said:

> Until now I have acted on the basis, that as a member of the court deriving its authority from the 1961 Constitution I was helping to safeguard the rights of citizens under that Constitution. It is my view that to continue in my office in the present circumstances, particularly in the light of the Government's declared intention not to recognise any right to appeal to the Privy Council, amounts to accepting abandonment of the 1961 Constitution . . . This renders nugatory the protection which the court can afford to rights enshrined in the 1961 Constitution. I cannot accept this abandonment with all that it entails, and accordingly I do not feel that I can continue as a member of the court.[29]

---

[27] Sir Hugh Beadle was a Privy Counsellor. As such he had undertaken to be a true and faithful servant of the Crown, not to countenance any word or deed against the Sovereign but to withstand the same to the utmost of his power, to bear faith and allegiance to the Crown and to defend its jurisdiction and powers. See *Halsbury's Laws of England*, 4th edn (1974) vol 8, para 1149.

[28] *Eshugbayi Eleko v Officer Administering the Government of Nigeria* [1931] AC 662, 670.

[29] Quoted in B Goldin, *The Judge, the Prince and the Usurper* (New York, Vantage Press, 1990) 122–23. The author (one of the judges sitting in the *Madzimbamuto* case in the High Court) also reproduces, at 95, a remarkable personal letter from Erwin

The rest of the story can be quickly told. The Smith government remained in office, fighting a debilitating and unwinnable guerrilla war, until 1978. A settlement in London brought independence and majority rule to the new Republic of Zimbabwe in 1980. The first Chief Justice of the new Republic was, fittingly, Fieldsend J. He and his successors maintained the independence of the courts against an increasingly unruly executive. Two years ago Gubbay CJ was compelled to leave the Bench, under threat of forcible removal. The rule of law in Zimbabwe has virtually gone.

I seek no moral in the present state of Zimbabwe. One cannot attribute the present lawlessness to Mr Smith's revolution, nor to the acquiescence in it of the Rhodesian judges. Nor is there any reason to think that if not for UDI President Mugabe would have been a more benign ruler.

But there may be a moral in the story of the Rhodesian judges. In any country with an independent judiciary there will always be some tension between the executive and the judiciary. Sometimes there will be pressure on the judiciary to pay special heed to the difficulties of government. The Rhodesian experience perhaps teaches us that any yielding to such pressures, whether on the plea of avoiding chaos, preserving peace or some lesser ground, may be the first step on a slippery slope. Such pressures, whether from government or the press or sections of the public, must be valiantly resisted. Not long ago, after a judge had given a decision most unwelcome to the government, the judge was savaged by a section of the press, and an angry minister said that he was fed up with a situation where Parliament debates issues and judges then overturn them. 'Parliament,' he said, 'did debate this and we are going to implement it.'

Neither the newspapers nor the minister were Zimbabwean.

My final word is that we should never assume that the independence of the judiciary is anywhere unassailable. It depends first on the integrity of the judges, which in this country we do not doubt, next on restraint observed by government, but equally

N Griswold (Solicitor General of the United States and formerly Dean of the Harvard Law School) to Sir Hugh Beadle. In one passage in this letter Dean Griswold wrote 'Under the law which gives you your judicial powers, the present regime is patently illegal de jure. While you hold the Queen's Commission I do not see how you can properly hold otherwise, and this makes everything else irrelevant. This is not a case of considering the effect of actions by a de facto government, after the event, where the de facto nature of the regime would be relevant. This is a case of the validity of the regime now, with the legal validity – not the de facto nature of its power – directly in issue. On that, I must confess that I can see only one conclusion, and it has always seemed to me that way.'

on the support that we as citizens give to the judges in their exercise of their vital constitutional function.

POSTSCRIPT

Daniel Madzimbamuto was released from detention in 1974 and went into exile in Zambia. He was a leading member of the Zimbabwe African People's Union (ZAPU) of Mr Joshua Nkomo. After independence in 1980, Mr Madzimbamuto continued to be active in ZAPU. He did not hold any political office, but until shortly before his death in 1999 he was Director of Postal Development for Zimbabwe. He is buried in Zimbabwe's Heroes' Acre.

Mrs Stella Madzimbamuto, a nurse, became a hospital matron. She retired in 1993. After her husband's death she moved to Cape Town, which was her birthplace.

~

8

The Highest Court:
*Selecting the Judges**

~

G
REAT HONOUR AS it is, it is nonetheless daunting to deliver the Sir David Williams Lecture in the presence of Sir David himself, and on a subject close to his own interests. The ideal David Williams Lecture would obviously be a lecture given by David Williams. But as that is not to be – at any rate, not this evening – my lecture, by definition then not the ideal lecture, will I hope be received as at least a personal tribute to an inspiring constitutional lawyer.

The highest court of the United Kingdom is not, strictly, a court at all. It is merely a committee of the House of Lords, the Appellate Committee. It sits ordinarily in a committee room in the House. As it is a committee, and not a court, its members do not sit in judicial robes or on a raised judicial bench, but unrobed at a table. The members of the Appellate Committee are full members of the House of Lords who are entitled to participate in the legislative processes of that House. Nonetheless, the core members of the Appellate Committee are full-time salaried professional judges, with the tenure and other rights of English High Court judges.[1] There are twelve of them, known as Lords of Appeal in Ordinary or, less formally, Lords of Appeal or the Law Lords. They are appointed by the Queen on the advice of the Prime Minister, who will have had one or more names recommended to him or her by the Lord Chancellor. The Law Lords constitute the final court

---

* This was the second Sir David Williams Lecture, given at Cambridge University in May 2002.
[1] 'Core' members, because retired Lords of Appeal in Ordinary may continue to sit on the Appellate Committee until the age of seventy-five. More rarely, a peer of the realm who has held 'high judicial office' may be invited to sit. Lord Cooke of Thorndon, formerly President of the New Zealand Court of Appeal, is a recent example.

of appeal for the whole of the United Kingdom. Appeals come to them from the Court of Appeal in England, the Inner House of the Court of Session in Scotland, and from the Court of Appeal of Northern Ireland.

Lord Justice Asquith, later himself a Law Lord, once described the qualities of an ideal trial judge. That judge, he said, was expected to be quick, courteous and right. This did not mean, he added, that the Court of Appeal was to be slow, rude, and wrong, for that would be to usurp the function of the House of Lords. These days, the House of Lords, judicially, is seldom slow and never rude. Appeals are heard and judgments given with reasonable despatch. As to being right or wrong, views on individual decisions obviously differ, but on the whole the practising profession is well satisfied with the work of the Law Lords. Now, and at least for many years past, the Appellate Committee has been intellectually impressive, impartial, fair minded, and, I believe, open minded. It would be too much to expect that every appointment of a Law Lord should receive a 100% endorsement from the legal profession (in which I include judges, practitioners, and legal academics), but in my time at the English Bar no appointment has caused major controversy, still less scandal. No plainly, or even arguably, unqualified judge has been promoted to the Lords. Nor, whatever government has been in power, has there during this time been any suggestion of political bias or preference in making the appointments.

Why, then, has there been in recent years a flow of books, articles, research papers, and speeches questioning and indeed radically challenging the present arrangements under which the judges of our highest court are appointed and do their judicial work? Writers and speakers question whether the present qualifications for appointment to the highest court are appropriate. Should candidates, they ask, be sought from a wider pool? Should the appointments remain in the hands of the executive? Should our highest court become solely a constitutional court? All these issues are being debated with different degrees of vehemence. Possibly my favourable assessment of the present performance of the Law Lords is wildly wrong. But if not, what has given rise to the calls for reform?

There is at present a fashion for general criticism of the judiciary, not particularly directed at the House of Lords. It may have something to do with the millennium. We are told that we must have judges fit for the twenty-first century. Our judges, it is pointed out, are mostly white, middle-class, middle-aged males. They are therefore said to be out of touch with ordinary life, and not representative of our diverse population. They are appointed by a secretive process lacking transparency and democratic legitimacy.

There are three particular issues which have, I believe, fuelled the debate about the Law Lords. The first is the peculiar constitutional position of the Lord Chancellor. He is a cabinet minister in charge of a department, and a legislator in the House of Lords, where he propounds and defends government policy. At the same time, he is a judge – indeed, the head of the judiciary. He may, if he chooses, sit on the Appellate Committee in any appeal, and when he does so he presides. But, unlike other judges, he has no security of tenure: he may be at any time removed from office by the Prime Minister. As a cabinet minister, he appoints all English judges below the Court of Appeal. Court of Appeal judges and Law Lords are nominated by the Prime Minister for appointment by the monarch. In reality, therefore, the power of appointment is with the Prime Minister, and it may be assumed that he generally acts on the advice of the Lord Chancellor. The judicial aspect of the Lord Chancellor's office has been attacked as a departure from the constitutional doctrine of the separation of powers, and as possibly incompatible with the European Convention on Human Rights. The attack has come not only from the less exalted ranks of the profession, but also most recently and most powerfully from one of the sitting Law Lords.[2] The desirability of the Lord Chancellor's triple role is not my theme this evening. I content myself with saying that the arguments are by no means all on one side. At all events, the controversy has naturally led to an examination of the Lord Chancellor's position as the de facto selector of the Law Lords.

The second issue is the call to separate the highest court completely from the House of Lords and to transfer its judicial functions to a newly created Supreme Court of the United Kingdom. The arguments for the change are partly constitutional – the separation of the judicial from the legislative power – and partly practical. The practical aspect is that the Law Lords are physically tucked away in the uncomfortable interstices of the House of Lords. It is said that when, a few years ago, an addi-

[2] Lord Steyn in his Neill Lecture, given at All Souls College, Oxford, on 1 March 2002. See also D Woodhouse, *The Office of the Lord Chancellor* (Oxford, Hart Publishing, 2001) *passim*.

tional Law Lord was appointed, a lavatory had to be converted into an office for him. A Supreme Court of the United Kingdom would merit a dignified and commodious building of its own, comparable to the Supreme Court buildings in Washington, Ottawa, or Canberra. Whether it follows that the highest court should no longer be part of the House of Lords is another question which I shall leave unanswered. This issue too has concentrated attention on the position of the Law Lords.

The third issue is one which truly warrants a reconsideration of all aspects of the appointments to our highest court. This is the passage of the Human Rights Act 1998, which made the European Convention on Human Rights an integral part of United Kingdom law, and thus gave us what is in effect, if not in name, a bill of rights. It has given to British judges a power which they have not previously claimed, and which permits and requires hitherto unknown judicial interventions not only in the sphere of executive action but also in the sphere of legislation. Indeed, it was this prospect which provided the principal argument for those who opposed the incorporation of the European Convention into our law. Thus Lord Mackay of Clashfern, when Lord Chancellor, said in a speech in 1996 that incorporation of the Convention:[3]

> would inevitably draw judges into making decisions of a far more political nature. The question which would then be asked, is whether the introduction of such a political element into the judicial function would require a change in the criteria for appointment of judges, making the political stance of each candidate a matter of importance. Following on from that is the question . . . whether their appointment should be subjected to political scrutiny of the sort recently seen in the United States.

I do not believe that the Human Rights Act has so far politicised our judiciary. Nor do I think that it is likely to do so in the manner feared by Lord Mackay. One must remember that even before the Human Rights Act judgments of English courts not infrequently had considerable political consequences or at least aroused acute political controversy. To mention only two, the decision of the Divisional Court restraining the government of the day from financing the building of the Pergau dam in Malaysia[4] and the decision of

---

[3] A speech to the Citizenship Foundation, Saddlers' Hall, London, 8 July 1996.
[4] *R v Secretary of State for Foreign and Commonwealth Affairs, ex parte World Development Movement Limited* [1995] 1 WLR 386.

the House of Lords in the case of General Pinochet.[5] But Lord
Mackay was not by any means wrong in pointing out that the
exercise of judicial power under an incorporated Convention could
now have a more directly political element. Before the Human
Rights Act, courts intervened to set aside an executive decision
only when they concluded that the decision was either illegal or
so irrational as to be outside the range of reasonable decision-
making. Now a reviewing court may be required to decide whether
the balance which a decision-maker has struck between individual
rights and a conflicting public interest was the correct one – a
decision which may have a decided political element. The Human
Rights Act does not give the courts the power to strike down
Acts of Parliament even if they are incompatible with the rights
embodied in the Human Rights Act. Parliamentary sovereignty
is thus preserved. But in introducing any bill into Parliament
the responsible Minister must now state that in his opinion the
bill either is, or is not, compatible with the Human Rights Act.
The negative option is likely to be rare. Consequently, while the
court's power is merely to declare an Act of Parliament to be
incompatible with the Human Rights Act, such a declaration may
have adverse political repercussions for the responsible minister
and his government. The devolution of powers to Scotland is also
likely to give rise to disputes which, under the relevant legislation, may end up in the Judicial Committee of the Privy Council.
As that Committee is largely (although not entirely) made up of
Law Lords or former Law Lords, there is further scope for judgments which may have a direct political effect.

These considerations have led some legal commentators to ask
whether the qualities and qualifications hitherto looked for in
a Law Lord are still the right ones. The formal qualifications
are simple – either two years experience of high judicial office
or a qualification to appear as an advocate in any of the three
high courts of the United Kingdom, held for at least fifteen years.
Of course, in reality rather higher qualifications are needed. All
the present Law Lords have been promoted from one or other of
the three courts of appeal in the United Kingdom. All of them
had been practising barristers before their first appointments as
judges. While the minimal statutory qualifications are the only
legal fetters on the Prime Minister's choice of new Law Lords,

---

[5] *R v Bow Street Metropolitan Stipendiary Magistrate, ex parte Pinochet Ugarte
(No 3)* [2000] 1 AC 147.

there is a firmly established convention that there should be two Scottish Law Lords. And since 1988 there has always been a Law Lord from Northern Ireland.

So much for the qualifications. What are the qualities hitherto looked for in a Lord of Appeal? The only publicly stated criterion is merit. Where a vacancy occurs the Lord Chancellor will recommend to the Prime Minister the person who appears to him the best qualified, regardless of gender, sexual orientation, ethnic origin, or religion – and, of course, regardless of political affiliation. That tells us what is not relevant. To define merit is more difficult. In this context, it must surely include outstanding intellectual ability as a lawyer, a judicial temperament, a sense of fairness, and considerable experience of the law in practice. I believe that those are the qualities that recent Lord Chancellors have looked for and, allowing for human error, have largely found.

It must at once be conceded to the critics that the Appellate Committee which merit in this sense has provided for us can hardly be said to be in any general sense representative. All its members stem from the practising profession, and all had served for many years as judges. They are all white men and, if 'middle-class' today means anything, I suppose they are all middle-class. They would, I think, confess to being middle-aged, some more cheerfully than others. For my part, I do not understand the call for a court to be representative. We are never told what sort of representation is contemplated or how it is to be achieved. Presumably no one in this country wants judges to be elected.[6] On the United States Supreme Court, I understand, it is essential to have a spread of Justices from different regions of the country. There is also now said to be a woman's slot on the Court, a Jewish slot, an Afro-American slot. and an Italian-American slot. It is said, too, that President Bush is now looking to appoint a Hispanic-American when next a vacancy occurs. I do not believe that anyone here could seriously advocate that type of representation.[7]

[6] Dame Brenda Hale (Lady Justice Hale) has written that 'judges should be no less representative of the people than the politicians and civil servants who govern us', but she nonetheless disavows any suggestion that judges should be elected: B Hale, 'Equality and the Judiciary' [2001] *Public Law* 489, 503.

[7] I once heard the argument for representativeness pressed to its limits. I was in Washington DC when Judge Carswell, a Florida judge, was nominated for appointment to the Supreme Court by President Nixon. The American Bar Association, which assesses all candidates for Federal judicial office, had reported that Carswell was 'mediocre'. A western senator, riding to his rescue, said to the Committee that there

The concept of representativeness may be quickly discarded. A more fruitful concept is diversity. Diversity in a court of final appeal is in my view a good in itself. This does not mean that a woman judge on the panel or a judge from a different ethnic background will necessarily decide a case differently from a white male judge. But their presence could enrich the court. The case for diversity was put this way in a recent article by Lady Justice Hale (one of only three women who have so far reached the English Court of Appeal):

> a generally more diverse bench, with a wider range of backgrounds, experience and perspectives on life, might well be expected to bring about some collective change in empathy and understanding for the diverse backgrounds, experience and perspectives of those whose cases come before them.[8]

I am certain that this is true. I speak from my experience as an acting justice of the South African Constitutional Court. It was a court the like of which had, needless to say, never before been seen in South Africa, and I doubt whether such a court has been seen anywhere else. Of the eleven judges on the court, there were six white men, three black men, one black woman, and one white woman. Five had been high court judges, some had come directly from the Bar, and at least four had at some time been academics, as well as having practised as either advocates or attorneys. One had been a political exile. They were all good lawyers. But what I found overwhelming was the depth and variety of their experiences of law and of life. This diversity illuminated our conferences especially when competing interests, individual, governmental, and social, had to be weighed. I have no doubt that this diversity gave the court as a whole a maturity of judgment it would not otherwise have had. Yet no one, black, white, male, or female, was representing any constituency. The South African Constitution states only that the need for the judiciary to reflect broadly the racial and gender composition of the country must be considered when judicial officers are appointed.[9] That was achieved.

The South African Constitutional Court was an entirely new court, established under a constitution that was a deliberate break with the past. Bringing an element of diversity into our highest

---

were a great many mediocre people in the United States, and that they too were entitled to their representative on the court. (Carswell was not confirmed.)

[8] [2001] PL 489, 501.

[9] The Constitution of the Republic of South Africa Act, No 108 of 1996, s 104(2).

court in the United Kingdom is a different problem. For practical purposes, the immediate issue is the absence of women on the court. In the nature of things, the judiciary is chosen from senior practitioners, among whom the proportion of women is still small. There are no more than a dozen women among the approximately 120 judges of the High Court in England and Wales. Three out of thirty-six members of the Court of Appeal are women. One of those three is the respected President of the Family Division, The other two, while also respected, are comparatively junior on that court. There are three women among the thirty-two judges of the Court of Session in Scotland, none as yet in the Inner House, which is the appellate court. As far as I know, there are no women in the higher courts of Northern Ireland. How long are we to wait for women judges to make their way up to the House of Lords? Can what has been called the trickle-up process be accelerated? Perhaps it can. Affirmative action is a distasteful expedient, if it means appointing a person not really up to the job, on grounds of gender or race. Among other things, it is humiliating for the person so appointed. But, if there is a choice to be made between a number of well-qualified candidates, to give deliberate prefer- ence to a woman among them is surely justifiable in the public interest, and would be for the long-term benefit of the court. It could theoretically fall foul of the jurisprudence of the European Court of Justice[10] – but choice of the best candidate has in any event an inescapable subjective element, and the selection of a well-qualified Lady of Appeal would, I hope, be applauded.

Given that the major task of a final court of appeal is to decide important questions of law, some writers have suggested that some diversity could be achieved by appointing senior legal academics direct to the highest court.[11] There is precedent for this in the United States. Justice Felix Frankfurter, who was transplanted by President Roosevelt straight from the Harvard Law School to the Supreme Court of the United States, had had no judicial experience. He subsequently gave a public lecture, celebrated or notorious in its time, which was in effect a defence of his own appointment.[12] His theme was that the work of the US Supreme

---

[10] See *Kalanke v Freie Hasestadt Bremen* [1995] IRLR 660; *Marschall v Land Nordr- hein Westfalen* [1998] IRLR 39.

[11] See, eg A Le Sueur and R Cornes, *The Future of the United Kingdom's Highest Courts* (London, School of Public Policy UCL, 2001) 115.

[12] 'The Supreme Court in the Mirror of Justices', the first Owen J Roberts Memorial Lecture, given at the University of Pennsylvania Law School. Justice Frankfurter said

Court was so different from that of other courts that prior judicial experience was an irrelevance.

It is not for me to say that the eminent Justice was wrong, but his words certainly have no application to the House of Lords. The Appellate Committee, unlike the US Supreme Court, has to deal with the whole field of private as well as public law. Nor is its work merely to solve legal conundrums. There are few appeals which do not entail a careful study of the facts and, often, an understanding of the processes and strains of litigation. A Law Lord with neither prior judicial experience nor long years in practice would be at a considerable and possibly incurable disadvantage. Besides, judicial qualities are best assessed through performance on the bench in the lower courts. Of course, there have been notable exceptions. English Law Lords have occasionally been appointed directly from the Bar. The last of these, Lord Radcliffe, was so appointed by Mr Attlee in 1949 – but Lord Radcliffe was a QC of great experience and exceptional brilliance.[13]

I must make it clear that I am certainly not against the appointment of academics to the bench. But I believe that they should come to judicial office by the same route as practising barristers or solicitors. Some academics have become recorders and in appropriate cases sit as deputy High Court judges. I hope and expect that some of these appointments will lead to a full-time judicial career, with every prospect of promotion on merit to higher courts.

Wherever the Law Lords come from, whatever their gender, the question remains – in the era of the Human Rights Act, should we look for different qualities in our top judges? Sensitivity to social issues and an appreciation of the importance of individual rights would be desirable qualities – if only there were some way of discerning them. Perhaps the best we can hope for is that a marked absence of those qualities will disqualify. About two years ago a Scottish judge was engaged in an appeal in which the appellants had invoked their rights under the European Convention. Before the conclusion of the appeal the judge published articles in the press roundly attacking the incorporation of the Convention into United Kingdom law. He suggested that the Convention would provide 'a field-day for crackpots, a pain in the neck for judges and legislators and a goldmine for lawyers'.[14] I have no

---

that 'the correlation between prior judicial experience and fitness for the functions of the Supreme Court is zero'.

[13] I shall refer below to the political exceptions.

[14] See *Hoeckstra v HM Advocate (No 3)* [2000] HRLR 410, in which another Scottish

reason to think that the learned judge aspired to the House of Lords, but one would hope that such views would be a positive disqualification for highest judicial office. Affirmatively, I would suggest that experience of public law should count more heavily. Broad jurisprudential interests will be more desirable than ever. Some suggestions have gone further. Sir Thomas Legg QC, the former Permanent Secretary in the Lord Chancellor's Department, whose knowledge of the judicial appointment process, and of the judiciary, is unequalled, has written that with the 'advent of the new era' (ie the human rights era) there is a case for 'enlarging the courts' political understanding and horizons' by appointing some lawyers, whether academics or practitioners 'with experience of public life'.[15] Professors Le Sueur and Cornes, in their indispensable research paper, 'The Future of the United Kingdom's Highest Courts',[16] speak of the desirability of judges at the highest level having political astuteness, and the 'requisite political skill', in a 'broad, non-partisan sense'. They say:[17]

> There is an argument that the process of wringing politics out of the appointments process in the last 20 years or so [I would say in the last 40 years or so] has left the senior judiciary over-insulated from the political world.

It is difficult to disagree with those views in the abstract. But the problem is to define political astuteness even, or especially, in the 'broad, non-partisan sense', and to identify those who have it. As far as I am aware, none of the present High Court judges has been a Member of Parliament. And it is now rare for leading lawyers to enter the House of Commons. It was not always so. In the nineteenth century, and well into the twentieth century, judicial appointment was a well-recognised reward for party political services. Research carried out by Professor Harold Laski, for his 1932 essay 'The Technique of Judicial Appointment,[18] established that, between 1832 and 1906, out of the 139 judges appointed in the period, eighty were Members of Parliament at the time of their appointment and another eleven had stood as candidates for Parliament. Up to the time of the Second World War, the Attorney-General and Solicitor-General of the day had by conven-

appellate court set aside the decision of the court of which that judge had been a member.

[15] 'Judges for the New Century', [2001] *Public Law* 62, 69.
[16] See above n 11.
[17] Ibid, 113.
[18] Published in *Studies in Law and Politics* (London, Allen & Unwin, 1932).

tion the reversion of the highest judicial offices, as vacancies came up. In that era the convention was accepted. It led, indeed, to the appointment of some of our most eminent judges. The formidable nineteenth-century Master of the Rolls, Sir George Jessel, was Solicitor-General when appointed. Lord Macnaghten, elevated to the House of Lords in 1887 from the unpromising springboard of Attorney-General for Ireland, was possibly the most brilliant Law Lord of his time. But these political appointments came to be questioned. When, in 1923, Sir Ernest Pollock, a not particularly impressive Solicitor-General, was appointed Master of the Rolls, there were protests in the press and from the legal profession. I must, however, add that, after he had sat in his first appeal, counsel who had been in his court was eagerly asked by his colleagues for his impression of the new Master of the Rolls. 'Disappointingly good,' he reported. No such story palliates the appointment of his contemporary Lord Hewart, the Attorney-General who was made up to Lord Chief Justice in 1922, and held that office until 1940. Mr RFV Heuston, that most learned and critical historian of the judiciary, expressed the considered opinion that Hewart was the worst Chief Justice England had had since the end of the seventeenth century.[19]

In the 1940s and 1950s, a few politicians were appointed to the Bench and ultimately reached the House of Lords. Their ability and impartiality could not be questioned.[20] In Scotland, for reasons relating to the nature of the Scottish legal profession, Lord Advocates (in effect, the Scottish equivalents of the Attorney-General) have continued to be directly appointed to the higher judiciary, including the House of Lords. One of them was Lord Reid, one of the truly great judges of his time. But I have no doubt that the time has passed for transfers from politics to the Bench. Something may indeed have been lost, but more has been gained. To try to reintroduce undefined political experience as a qualification would be a step backwards on a slippery slope. Lord Salisbury, Conservative Prime Minister at the turn of the twentieth century (as reported by his daughter), said that, within certain limits of intelligence, honesty, and knowledge of law, one man would make as good a judge as another, and a Tory mentality was ipso facto

[19] RFV Heuston, *Lives of the Lord Chancellors, 1885–1940* (Oxford, Clarendon Press, 1964) 603.
[20] I have in mind Lord Somervell of Harrow, Lord Donovan, and Lord Simon of Glaisdale. There may have been others whom I have overlooked.

more trustworthy than a Liberal one.[21] Ours is a more fastidious age. We do not want to slide back in that direction.

A related question which has been raised by the Human Rights Act is whether our highest court ought to become solely a constitutional court, like the constitutional courts of Germany and some other European countries and, more recently, South Africa. For my part, I see no need for such a court in the United Kingdom. There were reasons of history in both Germany and South Africa, not entirely dissimilar, for a separate constitutional court under a new constitution which was intended to be a complete break with an oppressive past. Significant as the Human Rights Act is, it does not constitute the same sort of revolution. On a practical level, cases on human rights in the United Kingdom can seldom be categorised as purely constitutional cases. They usually entail consideration of the common law, both civil and criminal.[22]

The Law Lords, in my respectful opinion, have shown themselves fully capable of handling the jurisprudence which has developed from the European Convention on Human Rights, and have already demonstrated that human rights cases in this country do not call for a separate panel of human rights specialists. I should like to emphasise what is sometimes forgotten when we speak of the need for judicial sensitivity to human rights issues. A culture of rights does not mean that the individual must always win against the state, or that every individual right must be extended to its furthest limit. Human rights adjudication requires above all a sense of proportion and balance.

What remains to be considered is the manner in which the judges of the highest court are selected. It is in this context that we hear the words 'transparency' and 'democratic legitimacy'. As I have said, there are no formal constraints on either the Prime Minister or the Lord Chancellor in selecting the Law Lords. Needless to say, in recent times the Lord Chancellor has consulted very widely before making any recommendation. This is and has been his practice before making any judicial appointment. Again, Sir Thomas Legg is the invaluable source. For appointments at High Court level and above, the Lord Chancellor consults a small group of what Sir Thomas calls 'top judges'. There is also informal consultation, in some cases, with other branches of the

---

[21] Quoted in Heuston, above n 19, 37.

[22] As David Steel J remarked in a recent (unreported) case, 'The tentacles of the Human Rights Act extend into some unexpected places. The Commercial Court . . . is not immune.'

legal profession. A report by Sir Lionel Peach, the former Public Appointments Commissioner, has concluded that the Lord Chancellor's system was as good as any he had seen in the public sector – which I assume was intended as a compliment. I would agree with Sir Thomas' conclusion:[23]

> Like any system, this one should be judged by its results. Many, including most of its critics, accept that it has produced a judiciary of high overall quality. There is no serious suggestion that the power of appointment has been abused for political or other improper purposes.

As long as this system remains, its democratic legitimacy comes from the democratic accountability of the Prime Minister and the Lord Chancellor. As to transparency, the system itself is well known. And the appointments themselves are open to the judgment of the public. I can see only disadvantages in disclosing the reasons why the Lord Chancellor and the Prime Minister have preferred Lord Justice A to Lord Justice B for a vacancy in the House of Lords. Mr Marcel Berlins of *The Guardian* has extracted from the Public Records Office an entertaining account of the appointment of two new Law Lords by Mr Attlee in 1949. One name put up for consideration was Lord Merriman, then the President of the Probate, Divorce and Admiralty Division of the High Court. Soundings were taken by the Lord Chancellor and his permanent secretary, and their report was that:[24]

> Lord Merriman would be most unsuitable for promotion; that he has not the requisite capacity; and furthermore, that if he were appointed he would soon put up the backs of his colleagues and they would all be at sixes and sevens. So strongly does the Master of the Rolls [Lord Greene] take this view that if Lord Merriman were appointed, he (the Master of the Rolls) would be unwilling to accept a lordship of appeal and would prefer to stay where he is. By contrast both the Lord Chief Justice and the Master of the Rolls agree that Cyril Radcliffe would make an admirable lord of appeal.

So Merriman was not appointed, and Greene and Radcliffe were. What possible good would it have done either for Merriman or the appointment system if, in the name of transparency, the reasons for the Prime Minister's choice had had to be made public?

When I had reached this stage in the preparation of this lecture, I began to feel qualms, if not dismay. It seemed that, in a lecture

[23] Above n 15, 64.
[24] *The Guardian*, 20 March 2002.

given in honour of so creative and original a legal thinker as Sir David Williams, I was doing no more than defend the status quo. I fear that that has turned out to be largely true, but not entirely. The present system of selecting the higher judiciary, and especially the Law Lords, has a potential flaw, notwithstanding its successful outcomes in recent years. The flaw is that it depends so heavily on the judgment and integrity of the Lord Chancellor of the day. Lords Hailsham, Elwyn-Jones, Mackay, and Irvine, to name the four most recent Lord Chancellors who have made appointments to the Lords, have been impeccable in avoiding any hint of political favouritism or any basis of appointment other than merit. But that is no guarantee for the future, especially as it is not inconceivable that the role of the Lord Chancellor in government will change. If his judicial role were one day to disappear, a future Lord Chancellor might not even be a lawyer.

I firmly believe that the appointment of judges, including those of the highest court, should remain the responsibility of the executive branch of government. In some European countries, such as Germany, Spain, and Italy, the judges of the highest court, the constitutional court, are elected by the legislature according to varying procedures, which usually require a special majority vote. Those countries no doubt have good reasons for choosing that system, and it presumably works to their satisfaction,[25] but I do not think that election of judges by Parliament is a serious runner in this country. It would make judicial appointments the subject of political conflict or, no more creditably, of political deals.

Very much the same objections would apply to any attempt to introduce a parliamentary confirmation process akin to the American system (commanded by their Constitution) of requiring executive appointments of federal judges, including Justices of the Supreme Court, to be subject to confirmation by the Senate. The bitter public conflicts over the nominations of Judge Robert Bork (who was rejected) and Justice Clarence Thomas (who was confirmed) have diminished whatever attraction that system might otherwise have had for us.[26] The American system must have its advantages – I have been told that the process gives a

---

[25] I cannot refrain, however, from quoting a news item which I saw last month in an Italian newspaper: 'Not enough members of parliament showed up on Thursday afternoon to allow for a binding vote on the appointment of two judges to the Constitutional Court. The vacancies have remained unfilled for almost two years due to political bickering' (*Italy Daily*, 12 April 2002).

[26] One may perhaps apply to nominees to the US Supreme Court the current dictum on candidates for the US Presidency: 'Presumed innocent until nominated'.

certain confidence to the judges who have survived it – but again I do not think there is any real belief here that it is an exportable system.

A more promising suggestion is a judicial appointments commission. There are different models for such commissions, to be found in some European countries, in some states of the United States, in the Commonwealth, and now in Scotland. In some models it is the commission which actually makes the appointments, taking it out of the hands of the executive. In others, including Scotland, it merely makes recommendations to the executive. Another model is the Judicial Services Commission established by the new South African Constitution.

The political background to the South African Commission is essential to its understanding. At the time of the political changeover there was only one black judge and one woman judge. Moreover, during the 45 years of apartheid government the standing of the South African Supreme Court had been diminished by far too many appointments of judges whose only apparent qualification for the bench was their adherence to the party in power. The object of the Judicial Services Commission under the new Constitution was twofold. One was to prevent unmeritorious candidates being appointed on political or other improper grounds. The second was to encourage the transformation of the judiciary by the appointment of suitable black lawyers and women lawyers. Accordingly, the executive power of appointment has been fettered.[27] Where a vacancy occurs in any of the courts, including the Constitutional Court, judicial aspirants must apply to the Judicial Services Commission (or allow their names to be put forward by others). They must then appear before the Commission to be interviewed. It follows that the applicants are in open competition with one another. The sessions are open to the public and the press but are not televised. At the end of the process the Commission is expected to send up a shortlist of approved candidates for each vacancy. The President of South Africa may appoint any of those on the list or reject them all, but he may not appoint anyone not put up by the Commission.

The first requirement of any workable judicial service commission must be a composition which inspires confidence, and which is itself not solely in the hands of the executive. The South African

---

[27] The statutory provisions governing the functioning of the Commission are to be found in the Constitution of the Republic of South Africa Act, No 108 of 1996, ss 174 and 178. The Commission has established its own procedures.

Constitution makes elaborate provision to this end. The members include the Chief Justice (who presides); a Judge President of one of the provincial divisions of the High Court, designated by the other Judges President; two practising advocates (barristers), nominated by their profession; two practising attorneys (solicitors), similarly nominated; a teacher of law, designated by teachers of law at South African Universities; there are 10 parliamentary representatives chosen by the two houses of parliament in a way which ensures that opposition parties have equal representation; and four designated by the President as head of the executive after consulting all leaders of parties in the lower house of Parliament. Thus, while only seven members have to be lawyers or judges, one sees a genuine attempt to avoid government domination of the Commission.

Whether the Commission has fulfilled all expectations is debatable. I can only give my impression. I would say that it has succeeded in eliminating some poorly qualified candidates who might otherwise have hoped for political favour. It has not, in my opinion, been sufficiently rigorous in ensuring that legal knowledge and experience accompany the other qualities needed for the transformation of the judiciary. It is my opinion, too, that the non-legal members of the Commission have contributed little to the Commission's expertise. Yet, in general, I have no doubt at all that the Judicial Services Commission is in South African terms a huge advance on the old system of unfettered executive appointment. Notwithstanding the reservations which I have expressed, the South African experience convinces me that an independent commission would be a valuable addition to the process of selecting the judges of our highest court. I do not, however, think that we need a commission to select or nominate the judges on the South African model. Unlike South Africa, the United Kingdom does not face the problem of changing a system which was riddled with racial inequality and political and other forms of favouritism. Here the objective would be to ensure as far as humanly possible that non-political appointment on merit will continue to be the rule. What I suggest is a relatively small committee, whose sole functions would be to consider any appointment of a Law Lord proposed by the Lord Chancellor. The committee would receive in confidence all the material on which the Lord Chancellor had based his provisional choice, and would, if necessary, question him on why, for example, he prefers candidate A to candidate B. The committee should have the right to be consulted and to give advice, and should have the power for good reason to veto a proposed appointment. I would suggest that the majority of members be drawn from the active profession, by which I mean judges, barristers, solicitors, and legal academics, together perhaps with a recently retired Law Lord. There should be room for a senior civil servant, not in the Lord Chancellor's department, or another layman with experience of appointment processes in other contexts.[28]

I would avoid public hearings of any kind. The South African experience shows that public hearings, however courteously conducted, may be humiliating for rejected candidates, especially those who are already judges and have aspired to promotion. Competitive candidacy between judges is in itself distasteful and diminishes respect for the judiciary. In the light of calls for a public process, in the name of 'transparency', it is perhaps worth looking at some of the questions which have been put to candidates appearing before the South African Commission. There are sometimes searching questions about the candidate's activities and attitudes in both the old South Africa and the new. In one case a judge of very long experience who sought promotion was closely questioned about his previous membership to a secret society devoted to promoting Afrikaner nationalism and its ideology. In another case an application by a candidate who had been an industrial arbitrator was opposed by a party which had appeared before him in that capacity. The objection to his appointment was based on the allegation that his conduct at the arbitration had shown a disparaging attitude to women employees. He was interrogated in detail about his questions to witnesses and his findings. One may also recall the questioning of Robert Bork in the United States Senate Judicial Committee. He was called on to defend a decision that he had given as a Federal Circuit judge holding that a chemical company was entitled to require women employees to undergo sterilisation if they wished to continue in certain jobs. He was questioned about his part in dismissing the Watergate special prosecutor, Archibald Cox, fourteen years earlier.

It is not for me to say that in the contexts of South Africa and the United States such questioning was improper or unnecessary.

---

[28] The possibility of a commission to scrutinise all judicial appointments (which would be an enormous task) raises issues beyond the scope of this lecture. There is already an independent Judicial Appointments Commissioner who has no role in making actual appointments, but has power to scrutinise the processes of the Lord Chancellor's Department.

What these examples do show, I suggest, is how inappropriate, if not pointless, interrogation by a commission, even in private, would be in our judicial context. I would ask those who advocate the interrogation of candidates for high judicial office what sort of questions could usefully and properly be put to them. I cannot think of any. Although some judges, including Law Lords, may be popularly regarded as liberal and others as conservative, their views are not derived from party allegiance, if indeed they have any, nor from extreme ideologies, nor even from what Lord Mackay called a political stance. In this country, issues like abortion or the penalties for murder are not electoral issues and do not arouse the ferocious political debate that they do in the United States. When a new Law Lord is appointed there is no speculation on what his views will be on any issue likely to come before him. In England, unlike the United States, the judges of the highest court are not selected in order to satisfy particular political constituencies. Nor is there any equivalent here to the understandable South African sensitivity about a judge's pro-apartheid past. Naturally, a judge's ability as evidenced by his or her judgments would be taken into account in any selection process. But that judges should be called on to defend their judgments, even in committee, is not only distasteful but is, surely, incompatible with the independence of the judiciary. It cannot be justified by words like 'transparency' or 'accountability'.

This is a long path by which to have reached so modest a conclusion – Lords of Appeal to be appointed much as they are now, subject only to scrutiny and possible veto in extreme cases by an independent commission. This is not to disparage the research and thought of the observers of the House of Lords who have advocated more radical change. It is right that the court which is the ultimate protector of our liberties should be critically observed and appraised. But we should also keep in mind the limitations of institutional safeguards, whether simple or elaborate. In the end, we shall still have to rely on the wisdom, integrity, and good sense of the judges who sit in our highest courts.

POSTSCRIPT

As is well known, the House of Lords has ceased to be the final court of appeal. Its judicial functions were in 2009 transferred to the newly created Supreme Court of the United Kingdom.

The Law Lords became Justices of the Supreme Court. Newly appointed Justices are not peers, but have the courtesy title of Lord or Lady. The Lord Chancellor is no longer a member of the judiciary, but remains a cabinet minister in charge of the Department of Justice. The present (November 2012) Lord Chancellor is not a lawyer.

Aspirant Justices must now apply to a judicial appointments commission whose nominations go to the Lord Chancellor, who may reject a nomination but only on the ground that the nominee is not suitably qualified. The commission consists of the President and Deputy President of the Supreme Court and two lay members. Candidates are interviewed by the Commission. The questions put and the answers given are of course entirely confidential, but it may safely be assumed that they have no political content.

Since its inception, the Justices appointed to fill vacancies in the Supreme Court have with one exception been members of the Court of Appeal or (in Scotland) the Inner House of the Court of Session. The exception is Lord Sumption, who, like Lord Radcliffe in 1949, was appointed directly from the Bar. Also like Lord Radcliffe, he was a QC of great experience and exceptional brilliance.

Dame Brenda Hale was elevated to the House of Lords in 2004 as Baroness Hale, becoming the first Law Lady. She is now a Justice of the Supreme Court.

As to the South African Commission, the political element in its composition has been enlarged at the expense of the legal elements, with what consequences remains to be seen.

~

9

*Taking Liberties**

⁓

THE DELIBERATELY AMBIGUOUS title of this conference inevitably turned my thoughts back to South Africa at a time when the apartheid government was at its most powerful and oppressive. Laws provided for the forced removal of black communities from their homes to distant rural slums, no black person had the vote, there was compulsory racial segregation, and senior police officers had the power to detain any person whom they suspected of engaging in or having any knowledge of broadly defined 'terrorist activities' without trial or judicial warrant, without access to a lawyer or to a court, and for an indefinite period. Mr BJ Vorster, the Minister for Justice, later Prime Minister, irritated by a judgment which had struck down one of his regulations as being beyond even his vast powers, made a statement which achieved immortality. 'Rights,' he said, 'are getting out of hand.'

I could not have imagined that one day leaders of both the main political parties in the United Kingdom would be suggesting the same thing, if not quite as succinctly as Mr Vorster.

After the first suicide bombings in London, the Prime Minister, Mr Blair, said 'the rules of the game' had changed. Mr Cameron, as leader of the Conservative Party, has threatened to abolish the Human Rights Act.

Many organisations and individuals concerned with human rights have identified other reasons for concern – the broad sweep of the anti-terrorist legislation, the creation of new crimes such as 'glorifying terrorism', the introduction of control orders which may subject unconvicted suspects to what amounts to house arrest, the continuing pressure by the police for the extension of the time for

---

* This was the opening address at the Bar Conference in London in November 2007.

holding and questioning terrorism suspects beyond the present 28 days to 90 days.

The criticisms of or outright attacks on the Human Rights Act, together with the nature of the new anti-terrorism legislation, have led some people concerned with human rights to suggest that since 2001 there has been a concerted assault on our liberties. This was the theme of the film that was shown this morning before the official opening of the conference. I am told that it was sheer coincidence that the title of the film is *Taking Liberties*. It is a well-made and interesting film. It contains disquieting footage of heavy-handed police response to peaceful demonstrations, albeit in prohibited areas adjoining airfields or in the exclusion zone around Parliament. The film also shows the particularly unpleasant episode of the forcible expulsion from a Labour Party conference of a member who had done no more than shout out the one word 'nonsense', and his arrest under the anti-terrorism laws. These episodes led some of the people interviewed in the film to say that the right of peaceful protest has been lost in Britain. The film shows the conditions under which an unconvicted suspect is confined to his flat under a control order. It refers also to the one-sided extradition treaty with the United States, of which I shall later say more. And of course it quotes Mr Blair's dictum on the rules of the game.

The film concludes by saying that Britain may be on the way to becoming an authoritarian state where no one will be safe, and roundly asserts that over the past 10 years the basic liberties of this country have been successfully dismantled.

Any other view – any positive view of human rights in this country – seems to have escaped the makers of the film. You may say that this is just a privately made film, but the standing of some of the participants lends it some authority.

Of course, many of us share their concern at some of the episodes shown in the film, and we would have been happier if the theme of all the recent party conferences had been the extension and strengthening of the Human Rights Act. Nonetheless, human rights in a time of international terrorism is a subject which calls for some sense of proportion. The remarks of Mr Blair and Mr Cameron do not represent the fixed policies of their respective parties. The Home Office Minister for Security, Mr McNulty, has explicitly repudiated the idea that the rules of the game have changed. The present Prime Minister has foreshadowed a British bill of rights and duties which, it is said, will build on the best principles of the Human Rights Act, and will also make explicit the obligations of the citizen. Both he and Mr Straw have made it clear that they intend that the Human Rights Act will remain.

Notwithstanding Mr Cameron's remark, the Conservative Party's shadow Attorney-General, Dominic Grieve QC, has convened a committee of members of his party and others to consider the drafting of a British bill of rights. As I understand it, its remit is to build on, not to remove, present rights. Nor should the concept of in due course replacing the Human Rights Act with a home-grown bill of rights be treated with suspicion. The European Convention on Human Rights as incorporated into the Human Rights Act is not all-embracing. A British bill of rights might well cover such subjects as trial by jury, the right to vote, and the right to judicial review of executive action. It might also embody this country's anti-discrimination laws, which go far beyond anything in the European Convention.

As to the obligations of citizenship, it would be no bad thing to attempt to define them. Article 10 of the European Convention (Freedom of Expression) states that the exercise of that freedom carries with it duties and responsibilities. That is the only mention of duties in the Convention. What are the duties of a citizen? To pay taxes, to do jury duty – merely in general to obey the law? And what of the rights and duties of non-citizens who live here? It is worth further thought and discussion.

While recognising the real threat of terrorism, our judiciary has been protective of individual rights. I shall mention two cases among many. In *A v The Home Secretary (No 2)* the House of Lords ruled that no evidence obtained by torture would be admissible in any court or tribunal in the United Kingdom.[1] In *A v The Home Secretary* (the *Belmarsh* case) an order of the Home Secretary providing for the detention of non-nationals on suspicion of being terrorists was struck down by the House of Lords on the grounds that it was discriminatory and disproportionate.[2] Lord Bingham emphasised that the Court's role under the Human Rights Act as the guardian of human rights was a responsibility from which it could not abdicate.

Looking about us, we see that this country has no Guantanamo Bay. We have nothing on our statute book like the USA Patriot Act – an acronym: in full, an Act for 'Uniting and Strengthening

---

[1] *A v Secretary of State for the Home Department (No 2)* [2006] 2 AC 221.
[2] *A v Secretary of State for the Home Department* [2005] 2 AC 68.

America by Providing Appropriate Tools Required to Interrupt and Obstruct Terrorism'. Nor do we speak of 'the war on terror'. Our executive has never asserted the powers granted by Congress to President Bush, still less those exorbitant powers claimed by him. I have noticed no inhibition on criticisms of the government by its political opponents, by demonstrators, or by the press. Habeas corpus (contrary to an assertion in the film) has not been abolished by the 2005 Anti-Terrorism Act.

What, then, is one to say of the assertion that our basic liberties have been successfully dismantled? Heeding my own recommendation to approach these issues with a due sense of proportion, I would echo the heckler at the Labour Party conference: I would simply call it nonsense.

There are many well-known sayings about liberty. Here are two of them.

The price of liberty is eternal vigilance.

Yes, but vigilance does not mean alarmism.

Extremism in the cause of liberty is no vice.

No vice, but sometimes counter-productive because it devalues the liberties which we have.

I hope that does not sound too complacent. There are indeed issues that we as lawyers should be particularly concerned about. A major concern is the government's continuing pressure to increase the period for which terrorist suspects may be held before being charged or released. When the government first put the 90 day period to Parliament it was defeated by members of all parties in both Houses – surely a triumph for parliamentary democracy. Internationally based terrorism, aimed at civilians and carried out by suicide bombers is a new criminal activity in this country. It would be obtuse not to recognise that it is exceptionally difficult to detect and investigate. On that basis, the present period of twenty-eight days was found by Parliament to be justifiable. It is perhaps to be expected that the police would like more. In apartheid South Africa the police were given power to detain suspects for ninety days. Then they were given 180 days. Then, on the principle that all power is delightful, and that absolute power is absolutely delightful, they asked for and were given the power to detain indefinitely. While the police here would like ninety days, Mr Brown said last week that he would propose fifty-six days. One hopes that Parliament will consider that proposal not merely critically but sceptically. If any extension is granted one hopes that Parliament will insist on the closest judicial supervision.

Now I should like to speak particularly about the right to a fair trial – one of the rights in the Convention which I have always thought of as absolute (the other two are the right not to be tortured and the right not to be enslaved). Under the new system of control orders, however, the absolute nature of that right has been put in issue.

After the *Belmarsh* case, Parliament introduced an Act under which the Home Secretary may make a control order imposing restrictions on any person reasonably suspected of terrorism-related activity. In marked contrast to the Second World War regulation which gave rise to the case of *Liversidge v Anderson*,[3] the Home Secretary must satisfy a judge of the objective reasonableness of the suspicion, and the person affected is entitled to challenge the order before a judge. But there is a snag. The person affected is not entitled to know the reasons for the making of the Control Order, nor its factual basis, if disclosure would be contrary to the public interest.

The potential unfairness of that proviso, standing alone, was not overlooked by Parliament. To mitigate that unfairness, a special advocate who has had security clearance is appointed to assist the affected person. The special advocate has access to the government's confidential material, and may make submissions on it and may cross-examine the officers who have produced it. But that takes place in a closed session from which the affected person and his own advocate are barred. Nor may the special advocate disclose to them anything at all about the confidential material. The special advocate procedure constitutes, I have no doubt, a genuine attempt to reconcile fairness to the suspect with the public interest in confidentiality. But how has it worked in practice? In one case, where neither the essence of the allegations nor any factual basis for the suspicion was disclosed to the affected person, the judge held nonetheless that the special advocate procedure was sufficient to ensure fairness.

Fortunately, the case went to the House of Lords and judgment was given last Wednesday.[4] The majority judgments, and particularly that of Lord Bingham, restate the basic principle that a fair

[3] [1942] AC 206.
[4] *Secretary of State for the Home Department v MB* [2008] 1 AC 440.

trial, whether civil or criminal, requires that the affected person be informed of the charges and allegations which he has to meet. Lord Bingham, cited earlier cases in which Lord Hope had said that the Convention right to a fair trial was 'fundamental and absolute', did not admit of any balancing exercise and that the public interest could never be invoked to deny that right.[5] And in his concurring judgment last Wednesday, Lord Brown said:[6]

> I cannot accept that a suspect's entitlement to an essentially fair hearing is merely a qualified right capable of being outweighed by the public interest in protecting the state against terrorism (vital though, of course, I recognise that public interest to be). On the contrary, it seems to me not merely an absolute right but one of altogether too great importance to be sacrificed on the altar of terrorism control . . . closed material [must] be rejected if reliance on it would necessarily result in a fundamentally unfair hearing.

I should add two riders. It does not follow from the decision that every hearing under the special advocate procedure will necessarily be held to be unfair. Secondly, the judgments hold that, whereas house arrest for more than sixteen hours a day is unlawful as a deprivation of liberty under Article 5 of the Convention, anything up to sixteen hours will probably not be regarded as a deprivation of liberty, but merely as a restriction on the right of movement.

I consider the drawing of the line at sixteen hours most disappointing and, we have learnt, so does the Home Secretary, though for diametrically opposed reasons. Here I have another quotation which might be applied to both sides of the argument. It comes from the great American judge, Learned Hand. 'The spirit of liberty,' he said, 'is the spirit which is not too sure that it is right.'[7]

The right to a fair trial is also in issue in some current extradition procedures. The film *Taking Liberties* referred to the extradition treaty with the USA. Under this treaty, which has been given statutory effect here, in requesting extradition the United States does not have to provide prima facie evidence that the person accused has committed the alleged crime. This is one sided because the UK in seeking extradition from the USA does not have the same exemption. How this country put itself in this

---

[5] [2008] 1 AC 440, 476, [29].
[6] Ibid, 498, [91].
[7] Learned Hand, 'The Spirit of Liberty' address on 'I Am an American Day' (1944).

demeaning position has not, as far as I know, been explained. But even if it were a reciprocal rather than a unilateral provision it is still extraordinary. Extradition is not conviction, but it has drastic consequences for the accused person. It surely cannot be in accord with our conceptions of fairness that anyone should have to bear those consequences on the strength of a bald allegation.

The European Arrest Warrant also raises questions about fair trials. Each country in the European Union is now obliged, on receiving an arrest warrant issued by another Member State in respect of a wide variety of offences, at once to send the person named in the warrant for trial in the requesting state. Its introduction has been described by Lord Hope in the House of Lords as highly controversial because of 'a lack of confidence in the ability of the criminal justice arrangements of other member states to measure up to the standards of our own'.[8] That system, no part of our statute law, assumes that equal standards of fairness in criminal procedures prevail in all states of the European Union. That statutory assumption hardly cures the original lack of confidence. I may mention purely *obiter* that last month a judge in Florida refused to extradite an alleged gangster to one of the original members of the European Union because of a well-grounded fear that he would be tortured. Heretical as it may sound to European lawyers, I suggest that, on a showing of a real danger of unfairness abroad, the Human Rights Act may trump the European Arrest Warrant.

I have said that I believe that the right to a fair trial is, or should be, an absolute right. While there is no hierarchy of rights under the European Convention, I also believe that the right to a fair trial is in some ways the most important of the enumerated rights because it is that right which enables us to vindicate all the other rights. What is the most fundamental protection of the liberty of the individual in this country? I would say that it is the fact that any person charged with a criminal offence of any seriousness will be defended by an independent advocate of his choice, in a prosecution which will be conducted by another independent advocate before an independent judge. We may take that for granted, but I have known a system where it could not be taken for granted. That has taught me that it is not merely by great constitutional cases in the House of Lords that the rule of law in this country is vindicated; it is vindicated every time a

[8] *Office of the King's Prosecutor, Brussels v Cando Armas* [2006] 2 AC 1, 16, [23].

barrister goes into court to defend a client on a criminal charge. It follows that anything which undermines or devalues the work of the criminal bar undermines and devalues the rule of law.

I shall not attempt to draw up a balance sheet or a score card on the state of our liberties. My unsurprising summing up is that, while libertarians (among whom I include myself) have some causes for concern, on the whole our basic liberties have been defended and preserved notwithstanding the need to meet real and unprecedented terrorist threats. Disappointing as this conclusion may be to some, I discern no calculated assault on our liberties either by those who govern us or those who aspire to govern us.

So let us be vigilant and critical, but let us also be glad that we live and work in the United Kingdom.

I shall end with an anecdote. When I first came to the English Bar, something over twenty-five years ago, I naturally heard many stories about the great figures of the Bench and the Bar. One I particularly liked concerned Lord Goddard, the Lord Chief Justice, and John Foster QC. John Foster, in addition to being a great figure at the Bar, had been a Conservative MP and a junior minister. He was an early advocate of the adoption of the European Convention in this country. This was in the days when judges and barristers alike wore black jackets and striped trousers, and all wore either bowler hats or Homburgs. One day John Foster was crossing the Strand and he was not wearing a hat. He met Lord Goddard coming the other way. 'No hat, John,' said Lord Goddard. 'Free country, Chief,' said John Foster.

Let's do our best to keep it that way.

10

The Rule of Law:
*Ideals and Realities**

∽

I. INTRODUCTION

Y OU MAY WELL be wondering what more can at this
stage be said about the rule of law, with or without capital
letters. You may well think any further discussion by me
can produce nothing new, and when I have finished you will
probably feel that you were right. Nonetheless, a century and a
quarter after Dicey first placed the concept of the rule of law at
the heart of the United Kingdom's unwritten constitution, it has
remained a subject of debate. How is it to be defined? In an era
of constitutional instruments with explicit bills of rights, why do
we still need to use an expression so general and undefined as
'the rule of law'?

Yet use it we do. In the United Kingdom, the Constitutional
Reform Act 2005 provides in its first section that the Act does not
adversely affect 'the existing constitutional principle of the rule of
law'. In a case in the House of Lords in 2005, Lord Hope said 'The
rule of law enforced by the courts is the ultimate controlling factor
on which our constitution is based'.[1] Section 1 of the Constitution
of the Republic of South Africa (1996) includes among the values
on which the state is founded 'Supremacy of the constitution and
the rule of law'. Within the Commonwealth, these examples could
be multiplied. The concept has travelled far beyond the Commonwealth. The preamble to the European Convention on Human
Rights records that the governments of the European countries

---

* This was the keynote address delivered at the 17th Commonwealth Law Conference held in Hyderabad in February 2011.
[1] *R (Jackson) v Attorney-General* [2006] 1 AC 262, 304, [107].

which are parties to it have a common heritage of, among other things, the rule of law.

In the United Kingdom and, I think, elsewhere in the Commonwealth, the discussion of the rule of law has been reinvigorated by Lord Bingham, whose death last year deprived us of the greatest English judge of his generation. His celebrated Cambridge lecture of 2006 was later expanded in his book, *The Rule of Law*, published in 2010. I am, of course, indebted to that book. Today it is a natural starting point for any further discussion of the concept.

II. PARTIAL DEFINITION

Lord Bingham begins with what he calls a partial definition of the rule of law: 'all persons and authorities within the state, whether public or private, should be bound by and entitled to the benefit of laws publicly made taking effect (generally) in the future and publicly administered in the courts'.[2]

Lord Bingham called this only a partial definition because it says nothing about the content of those 'laws publicly made'. Taken alone, it would cover the publicly made laws of slavery as enforced in the southern states of the USA before the civil war or the apartheid laws of South Africa before 1994. Indeed, at one time the defence of the apartheid government to accusations that it flouted the rule of law was founded on a similar definition. Detention without trial or legal process, internal exile of whole black communities, enforced racial discrimination – all these measures were authorised by law. Mr BJ Vorster, Minister of Justice and later Prime Minister of South Africa, said in response to criticism of these infringements of the rule of law that there were as many interpretations of the rule of law as there were people. Mr Vorster could not be called an enthusiast for the rule of law.

I am not sure that we need worry about finding a precise definition. One recalls the dictum of Justice Potter Stewart in the United States Supreme Court in a case about pornography: 'I cannot define pornography, but I know it when I see it'.[3] On the whole, we know a rule of law state when we see it – or, at least, we know when the rule of law is absent. What is certain is that the content of what we mean by the rule of law has expanded. In modern times – say the last fifty or sixty years – there has been

[2] T Bingham, *The Rule of Law* (London, Allen Lane, 2010), 8.
[3] *Jacobellis v Ohio*, 378 US 184, 197 (1964).

a recognition that certain individual rights are 'fundamental', and deserve particular respect from executive, legislature, and the courts. This is true even of states within the Commonwealth which have no written constitution. In England, quite apart from the Human Rights Act, there has been judicial recognition (pioneered by Lord Justice Laws) that some common law rights were to be classed as fundamental. So it is no surprise that Lord Bingham fills out the concept of the rule of law by including in it respect for and enforcement of a now familiar bundle of fundamental rights.

III. HISTORICAL EXAMPLES

Lord Bingham gives a number of historical examples illustrating the development of the rule of law, mainly but not entirely in England. These include Magna Carta, the Petition of Right of 1628, which established that the king's order could not of itself justify an imprisonment, and the abolition of the Star Chamber in 1640, the practical effect of which was to abolish any judicial reliance on torture. It was only well into the next century that other European states abolished the practice. Of particular interest is the Habeas Corpus Amendment Act 1679, which outlawed the practice of sending prisoners to distant places beyond the reach of a writ of habeas corpus – a practice revived in this century by the United States in sending prisoners to Guantanamo Bay, a place not within the sovereignty of the United States and therefore, it was said, beyond the reach of habeas corpus. Fortunately, a majority of the Supreme Court rejected that argument, holding, in accordance with English authority cited to the court, that the availability of habeas corpus depended not on legal sovereignty but on the existence of actual power to imprison and release.

Lord Bingham's historical examples included the Act of Settlement 1701, which, by giving judges security of tenure, helped to establish their independence, and the adoption in 1789 of the Constitution of the United States of America. I should like to add two examples of my own of the rule of law in action. My first illustration is from England in the reign of Queen Anne. In 1708 a most unfortunate event took place in London. Blackstone tells the story. The Russian ambassador to England had been forcibly removed from his coach and arrested for a debt of £50 which he had incurred whilst in London. The ambassador was very soon released, but the Czar of Russia greatly resented this breach of diplomatic privilege as an affront to himself. The Czar was Peter the Great, no less, and he demanded that the Sheriff of Middlesex and all others concerned in the arrest should be punished with instant death. Queen Anne, through her secretary, sent a reply in memorable terms. The secretary was directed to inform the Czar that Her Majesty 'could inflict no punishment upon any, the meanest of her subjects, unless warranted by the law of the land: and she therefore trusted that His Imperial Majesty would not insist upon impossibilities'. This splendid reply no doubt astonished Peter the Great, who would hardly have understood the idea that a monarch's powers could be limited by law.

I go forward now nearly three hundred years, to the Republic of South Africa in the year 1998. The President of South Africa, Mr Nelson Mandela, had appointed a judicial commission to inquire into the administration of rugby football, a subject of great public interest in South Africa. The gentleman who then controlled the sport contested the validity of the appointment of the commission, alleging that the President had not properly considered the matter himself, as the relevant statute required, but had merely rubber-stamped the decision of a cabinet member. President Mandela filed a detailed affidavit showing that he had made the decision himself after full consideration of the facts. What happened next was that the judge in the case ordered President Mandela to appear in his court to be cross-examined on his affidavit. This order caused some shock, being seen as an affront to a revered President. It also caused considerable astonishment: not only was there no precedent for such an order against a head of state, but there was much precedent against it. (If I may venture a respectful opinion about the judge who made the order for the cross-examination, he was an unreconstructed relic of the apartheid regime.) Mr Mandela did not move a higher court to set the subpoena aside as he might have done. He did not claim executive privilege. On the contrary, whilst making clear his resentment of what he saw as a insult to his office, he stated that an order of court had to be obeyed by all persons, whatever their positions. He stood in the witness box in the open court room in Pretoria under cross-examination for five hours, answering the questions put to him with his customary dignity and courtesy. This was a leader and a teacher demonstrating to his country the meaning of the rule of law.

These examples were, each of them, great forward steps in the progress of civilization. Yet they constitute only a partial version of constitutional history. There is much to set against those victories for the rule of law. In the United Kingdom they did not prevent the Highland clearances of the early decades of the nineteenth century or the persecution of dissidents during and after the Napoleonic Wars. No rule of law restrained the travesties of justice perpetrated during those times by judicial monsters such as Lord Braxfield in Edinburgh. In 1772 Lord Mansfield, in the *Somersett* case, ruled that no person could be held in slavery in England.[4] Yet slavery continued to be practised and tolerated in British colonies for some sixty years more. The rule of law in the British overseas empire was in general what we might describe as attenuated. It did not prevent or punish the cruelties of Governor Eyre in Jamaica in 1865, nor the massacre committed by General Dyer at Amritsar in 1919. As late as the 1960s, among the last vestiges of direct colonial rule, we saw the forced removal of the small but long-established permanent population of the Chagos Islands, in order to accommodate a United States naval and airforce base on the island of Diego Garcia – an act of governmental injustice perpetrated by virtue solely of the royal prerogative without parliamentary or judicial authority.

The rule of law in the United States also had a fitful growth. The Declaration of Independence was a resounding affirmation of liberty under law: 'We hold these truths to be self-evident: that all men are created equal; that they are endowed by their Creator with certain inalienable Rights; that among these are life, liberty and the pursuit of happiness'. But in 1857, in the *Dred Scott* case, the United States Supreme Court held, with only one dissentient, that 'all men' did not include black men.[5]

IV. TERRORISM

Even in the modern era of democracy and human rights, governments have not found it easy to live up to the ideal of the rule of law. In the United States, after the terrorist outrages of September 11, 2001, the Bush administration reacted with measures such as indefinite detention of suspects without trial, interrogations under torture and stringent limitations on access to the courts. Within the Commonwealth, reactions have been less extreme.

[4] *R v Knowles, ex parte Somersett* (1772) 20 State Tr 1.
[5] *Dred Scott v Sandford*, 60 US 393 (1857).

There is, as far as I know, no equivalent to the 'Patriot Act', no Guantanamo Bay. But there have been controversial restrictive measures, which I shall say more about in due course.

The truth is that at no time and in no country can we take the rule of law for granted. In the Commonwealth, at least, this is not necessarily because our governments are wicked or authoritarian. Government in this age is a difficult task. In general, human rights are not absolute. They must be balanced against competing rights, and against other public interests. In the age of terrorism there are real threats to public safety. Those who govern us are not all-knowing; they grope for solutions. Sometimes their solution entails overriding individual liberties in favour of other public interests. The courts cannot always resist this. Indeed, honest and independent judges may accept the rationality of the legislature's view of the proper balance to be struck between conflicting rights.

This should not be too dispiriting. Realism is not to be taken as pessimism. The rule of law continues to have its successes as well as its setbacks. The struggle is an unending one. But in our commitment to uphold the rule of law we should not assume that our government and our legislators must be our enemies. Many, if not most, of the advances in the rule of law have come not from the courts but from the other branches of government. The United Kingdom's Human Rights Act is an obvious example. Nor does the rule of law require that judges should always find against the government.

Even in relation to the rule of law there is room for a sense of proportion. In an address which he recently gave on counterterrorism and the law, Arthur Chaskalson, the first President of the Constitutional Court of South Africa and former Chief Justice of South Africa, said this:

> Courts cannot be expected to carry the full burden of what might be required. In a democracy parliament and civil society are also defenders of the rule of law and it is essential that they should play their part in its protection.

V. JUDICIAL REVIEW

We tend to see the rule of law as depending on the process of judicial review. In the celebrated *Minerva Mills* case in the Supreme Court of India, Bhagwati J said that if there was one feature of the Indian Constitution which more than any other was fundamental to democracy and the rule of law it was the power of judicial review.[6] That great constitutional lawyer, the late Sir William Wade, wrote that the courts' inherent power of judicial review was the 'fundamental mechanism for upholding the rule of law'.[7] Nonetheless, as Mr Chaskalson said, the judges alone cannot be expected to bear the whole burden.

I believe that all but two of the members of the Commonwealth have written constitutions. These constitutions either expressly or by implication embody the power of judicial review. But written constitutions are not writ in stone. They may be amended, usually by vote of a special but not unattainable majority. I know that in the *Minerva Mills* case of 1980 and in several other cases the Supreme Court of India has held that certain of the rights embodied in the Constitution of India are so fundamental that Parliament's general power to amend the Constitution did not extend to such rights. Among the inviolable features that have been so identified are judicial review and the independence of the judiciary. I believe that the Supreme Court of Mauritius has, in a different context, also held there to be implied limitations on the legislature's power of amendment under the Mauritius Constitution. The reasoning in these cases is impressive. However, the vital point is that in India and Mauritius the legislative and executive branch accepted these rulings, or at least decided to avoid a conflict with the judiciary over them.

The political reality which a hard look at the world about us forces us to face is that, if a legislature or a government is sufficiently confident of popular support, and if the issue at stake is sufficiently important, it may risk a conflict with the judiciary or even in extreme cases (as in Fiji and Zimbabwe) replace an independent judiciary with one to its own liking. One of the authors of the American constitution famously said that the judiciary was the weakest, the least dangerous, branch of government: it possessed neither the sword nor the purse. Thus it must rely for its power on the respect and support of the other two branches and, ultimately, of the people whom they represent. As lawyers, it is therefore our special duty to foster and strengthen public respect and support for the judiciary in its role as guardian of individual liberty.

[6] *Minerva Mills Ltd v Union of India* (1981) SCR(1) 206, 216.
[7] HWR Wade and CF Forsyth, *Administrative Law*, 10th edn (Oxford, Oxford University Press, 2009) 30.

VI. RULE OF LAW AND DEMOCRACY

Is the rule of law separable from democracy? Dicey, writing on the rule of law in Britain in the late nineteenth and early twentieth centuries, took for granted the democratic nature of the British constitution, although universal suffrage in Great Britain only came some forty years after his great book on the law of the constitution was first published. You will not, I think, find the word 'democracy' in the index.

What he saw as distinguishing the English system from the system of government in European countries was not democracy but the fact that in England, at least from the end of the seventeenth century onwards, no person could lawfully be made 'to suffer in body or goods' except for a distinct breach of the law. Dicey's paradigm example was the treatment of Voltaire. The literary hero of France, as Dicey calls him, was in 1717 sent to the Bastille for a poem he had not written and whose author he did not know. A few years later he was viciously beaten by the servants of a noble duke in the presence of their master for some real or supposed affront. Far from having any redress, Voltaire, because he complained of this outrage, was again sent to the Bastille. This could not have happened in England.

Dicey, in the last edition of his book, writing in 1914, rather patronisingly (and, as we now know, extremely optimistically) said that in the twentieth century an English observer might well say of most European countries that the rule of law was nearly as well established there as in England. But, he continues, foreigners (his word) still rightly saw the absence of arbitrary executive power to be the essential characteristic of the English constitution.

In our world, however, it is difficult to visualise a state in which the rule of law exists in the absence of genuine democracy. In a lecture given at Oxford in 1951, Owen Roberts, a Justice of the United Supreme Court, said that the rule of law was an idea recognised by what he called 'highly civilised nations'. Asked what countries he would include in that category, he said:

> My test would be: first, a country that has a representative form of government; second, a country where individual liberty and freedom are protected by law; (third,) where there are bounds to what the government can do to an individual.[8]

---

[8] Discussion by Justice Owen J Roberts at Oxford following his lecture, 'The Rule of Law in the International Community' (1951), quoted in AL Goodhart, 'The Rule of Law and Absolute Sovereignty' (1958) 106 *University of Pennsylvania Law Review* 943.

This formulation, with democratic government as its starting point, is both attractive and realistic. Naturally it excludes from the category of highly civilised nations a number of states of considerable military and economic importance, including some which on other criteria could no doubt be regarded as civilised. I have not tried to make a list of such countries, but they include powerful and influential countries such as China, the Russian Federation, and Iran which, whatever their other claims to civilisation, fall outside Justice Roberts's definition.

Unhappily, even in countries which have democratic constitutions, civil unrest, ranging from local uprising to outright civil war, or even conditions of dire economic collapse, may make the yardstick of the rule of law seem irrelevant. This was a point forcefully made by Johan Kriegler, a former judge of the South African Constitutional Court and an internationally experienced observer and analyst of national elections. His subject was the rule of law in post-colonial Africa, based on his personal visits to and study of a number of countries. One of them was Sierra Leone. Since the ending of the civil war in that country, there had been three general elections and relative peace had prevailed. Nonetheless, Mr Kriegler summed up what he saw in these words:[9]

> In the absence of elementary essential services such as potable water, rubbish and sewage disposal, electricity and trafficable roads, the quality of life for most Sierra Leoneans is so abysmal that speaking of the Rule of Law verges on the obscene.

There are other countries, in more than one continent, whose problems go too deep to be analysed in rule of law terms.

VII. INDEPENDENCE OF THE JUDICIARY

There are some aspects of the rule of law on which, among ourselves, we take different views. Trial by jury is one of them. The death penalty is another. But one aspect of the rule of law on which we would certainly all agree is the independence of the judiciary. It is secured in part by laws which give the judges security of tenure and in part by ensuring as far as possible that they are persons of integrity, appointed on merit rather than by reason of political connection. Independence here means more than inde-

---

[9] Judge J Kriegler, 'The Rule of Law in Post-Colonial Africa: A British Legacy?', Second Annual Rule of Law Lecture, delivered at Gray's Inn on 3 December 2008.

pendence from government direction. It means also that judges in making their decisions should as far as humanly possible not be influenced by public opinion, or by any sense of obligation to the government or to any individual, party, or pressure group. There is a particular threat to judicial independence which should concern us: that is, the growing tendency for politicians and the press to attack in intemperate and even vituperative terms judges who have given decisions with which they disagree. Newspapers all too often respond to an unpopular decision with personal attacks on the judges concerned. Judges must accept strong criticism, even unfounded criticism. Lord Atkin's statement that justice is not a cloistered virtue has become a legal cliché. As Lord Judge, the Lord Chief Justice of England and Wales, has recently said, one of the attributes we expect of an independent judge is the moral courage to make decisions which will be unpopular with politicians or the media or the public.

Judges, it has also been said, must have broad backs, and usually they have. The real mischief of unwarranted attacks on the motives and integrity of the judges, however, is not any hurt to the judge's feelings; it is that they undermine that respect for the judiciary without which, as I have suggested, the foundations of the rule of law are undermined.

There is no easy remedy. Contempt of court in the form once known as scandalising the judges has in many Commonwealth jurisdictions fallen into disuse – although not in all, as the recent prosecution and imprisonment of a writer, Mr Shadrake, for his criticisms of the application of the death penalty by judges in Singapore has shown. In any event, contempt proceedings are an unattractive response to criticism of the judiciary. What we as a profession can do is to defend the judiciary in its constitutional function – as our colleagues in Pakistan, Uganda, Kenya, and elsewhere have tried to do.

VIII. FAIR TRIALS UNDER ANTI-TERRORIST LEGISLATION

There is another issue which concerns us in many of our countries – the effect on the rule of law of anti-terrorist legislation. I shall speak about the United Kingdom, not because it is unique, but because I am not qualified to discuss developments in other jurisdictions.

In summary, the problem which arises is that, on the basis of confidential intelligence, there may be good reason to believe that there is a real risk that a particular person may commit an act of terrorism but there is insufficient admissible evidence to charge him with any crime. The United Kingdom legislation provides that such a person may be made subject to a control order. A control order is made by a cabinet minister, the Home Secretary. Very briefly, it is a form of house arrest, of varying degrees of severity.

These orders are subject to challenge before a High Court judge. The affected party may be represented by an advocate, but the judge may hear and rely on evidence which on national security grounds is withheld from the party and his advocate. To mitigate the obvious unfairness of this procedure, special advocates are appointed to act in the affected party's interest; they have access to all the secret evidence, but they must not disclose it to the party or to his own advocate. The consequence has been that in some cases the person subject to the control order was told little or even nothing of the case against him.

There has been considerable litigation challenging the fairness of the special advocate procedures. The issue came down to this: did the affected person have to be told enough of the case against him to enable him to answer it effectively or could there be cases where the judge was satisfied that the secret evidence was so strong that no disclosure of it could make any difference. The House of Lords, following a judgment in the European Court of Human Rights, has (fortunately, all or most of us would say) rejected the latter proposition.[10] It has held that details of the secret evidence need not necessarily be disclosed, but the affected party has to be told at least the gist of the case against him – enough to enable him to give effective instructions to the special advocate. That is the irreducible minimum.

That position hardly represents the ideal of a fair trial under the rule of law. But there are some positive features. Bearing in mind that British courts have no power to strike down Acts of Parliament, they have acted vigorously yet thoughtfully to limit the departures from the rule of law. Further, the government and Parliament have accepted the decisions of the courts and have so far not attempted to overturn them by further legislation. A balance has been struck which represents a genuine attempt to reconcile the demands of public safety with the affected

---

[10] *Secretary of State for the Home Department v AF (No 3)* [2010] 2 AC 269.

individual's right to a fair procedure. That is some cause for satisfaction – but not, of course, for complacency. In his judgment in the House of Lords in the case about the special advocates' procedure, Lord Hope said this:[11]

> The consequences of a successful terrorist attack are likely to be so appalling that there is an understandable wish to support the system that keeps those who are considered to be dangerous out of circulation for as long as possible. But the slow creep of complacency must be resisted. If the rule of law is to mean anything, it is in cases such as these that the court must stand by principle.

IX. CONCLUSION

I would end as I began, with Lord Bingham. At the end of his book on the rule of law he asks the question, 'What makes the difference between good and bad government?' His own answer is this:[12]

> I would answer, no doubt predictably: the rule of law. The concept of the rule of law is not fixed for all time. Some countries do not subscribe to it fully, and some subscribe only in name, if that. Even those who do subscribe to it find it difficult to apply all its precepts quite all the time. But in a world divided by differences of nationality, race, colour, religion and wealth it is one of the greatest unifying factors, perhaps the greatest, the nearest we are likely to approach to a universal secular religion. It remains an ideal, but an ideal worth striving for, in the interests of good government and peace, at home and in the world at large.

That may stand as the testament of a truly noble and humane judge.

POSTSCRIPT

At present (November 2012), a bill to extend the special advocate procedure to civil and criminal proceedings is the subject of debate in Parliament and beyond.

～

[11] Ibid, 361, [84].
[12] Bingham, above n 2, 174.

11

*Evil under the Sun: The Death of Steve Biko**

~

ODAY IS THE thirty-fourth anniversary of the death of
Stephen Bantu Biko. He was thirty years of age. I read of
his death in the newspaper the following day. I had never
met him. Many, perhaps most, white people in South African had
never heard of him. I at least had heard of him as a militant
young black leader who espoused the Black Consciousness philosophy. And I had heard reports from some of my colleagues at
the Bar that as a witness for the defence at the trial in Pretoria
of some young black activists he had made a strong impression
on an initially unsympathetic judge. That was all. So I admit to
having been astonished at the extraordinary reaction to the news
of his death.

The bare facts, as they first came out, were that he had been
arrested for breach of a banning order confining him to the district
of King Williamstown, that he had been in the custody of the
Security Branch of the South African police at Port Elizabeth,
had become 'unwell', had been sent to Pretoria, and had died
there in a prison cell. I have said the reaction was extraordinary. Steve Biko was not the first man to have died while in the
custody of the Security Branch. He was, as far as these things
were known, the forty-fourth. But this death was reported internationally. In Washington the chairman of the Senate Foreign
Affairs Committee called the death an outrage. In the United
Nations it was described as tragic. In South Africa thousands of
black students demonstrated, with the usual hundreds of arrests.

* This was the annual Steve Biko Memorial Lecture, given at the University of
Cape Town on 11 September 2011.

Desmond Tutu, then Bishop of Lesotho, expressed the sense of loss felt within and beyond the black community. Chief Mangosuthu Buthelezi said 'only a country as mad as South African can waste such talent'.

The sense of outrage was hardly dampened by the first response of the South African government. The Minister of Police, Mr Jimmy Kruger, speaking in the congenial atmosphere of the Transvaal Congress of the Nationalist Party, stated that Biko had been on a hunger strike. One of the delegates, to the great amusement of his fellows, congratulated Mr Kruger for being so democratic that those who wanted to starve themselves to death were allowed by him to do so. Mr Kruger then made his never-to-be-forgotten statement 'I am not pleased nor am I sorry. Biko's death leaves me cold.'

There was, of course, no truth at all in the story of a hunger strike.

The wave of protest and condemnation did not die down. International pressure forced the Prime Minister, Mr Vorster, to promise a full enquiry. It took the form of an inquest, which opened two months later in Pretoria in the Old Synagogue – a deconsecrated building converted into a courtroom some years before especially to accommodate major political trials.

The Chief Magistrate of Pretoria presided at the inquest. There were several sets of advocates engaged – for the police, for the district surgeons who had attended Steven Biko, for the prisons department, and in addition the Attorney General. There were three of us representing the widow and the mother of Steve Biko – myself, George Bizos, and Ernie Wentzel. Our instructing attorney was the lively and efficient Shun Chetty. We were well prepared: we had been given all of the many affidavits made by members of the Port Elizabeth Security Branch, who had had custody of Steve Biko, and by the district surgeons and other doctors who had seen him. Further, the government pathologist had agreed that two pathologists who had been engaged on behalf of the family could observe and participate in the autopsy, which was carried out on the day after Steve Biko's death. The two pathologists were Dr Jonathan Gluckman and Professor Neville Proctor, an internationally known neuropathologist.

The inquest began on 14 November 1977 and ran for two weeks. I do not propose to tell the full story of the inquest. George Bizos has given a full masterly account of it in his book *No One To*

Blame.[1] It was well reported in the South African press. I shall try to give the essentials of what came to light at the inquest.

Steve Biko was arrested at a road block on 18 August, together with his friend Peter Jones. It is believed that they had been to Cape Town to visit political supporters. Steve Biko was taken to a Port Elizabeth prison and kept there until 6 September. On that day he was transferred to the headquarters of the Security Branch of the police, which were in a Port Elizabeth office building. He was held there for interrogation under section 6 of the Terrorism Act. There had been some inflammatory leaflets distributed in the Eastern Province and the Security Police presumably believed that he was responsible for them. In any event, they were anxious to induce him to admit some connection with them. No such connection was ever proved and those who knew Steve Biko best have always disputed it. At all events, on 6 September he did not tell the police anything they wanted to hear. On that day he was a fit and healthy man. On the morning of the 7 September he was seriously ill. He showed obvious signs of neurological damage, but he was never hospitalised. On the night of 12 September he was sent to a Pretoria prison. By the next morning he was dead.

There was never any doubt even before the inquest began of the cause of death. The story of a hunger strike was a clumsy fabrication. The cause of death was extensive brain injury caused by blows to the head. The pathologists, those employed by the state and those engaged by the Biko family, all agreed on this.

What, then, were the real issues at the inquest? First, the police throughout denied that Biko had been assaulted. Consequently, much of the police evidence was directed to finding some cause for his injuries which did not incriminate them. The second was the manner in which Steve Biko was treated throughout his detention.

On the first issue, there was a story to which all the officers who were present on the morning of the 7 September adhered. On that morning, Biko was taken from the mat on which he had lain all night under guard and in shackles and was taken to the interrogation room. There he was seated on a chair. When the major who was in charge of the interrogation began to question him, he sprang up and attacked the major with such fury that it took a captain who was also present and three other officers to

---

[1] G Bizos, *No One to Blame? In Pursuit of Justice in South Africa* (Cape Town and Bellville, David Philip Publishers and Mayibuye Books, 1998).

subdue him. In the course of that violent struggle, so it was said, he must have bumped his head on the wall and fallen to the floor, fighting furiously throughout. After he was brought under control he was taken back to his mat, where he was again placed in leg irons. He had so far made no statement and, on the evidence of the officers, he never thereafter spoke intelligibly. That bump against the wall was the cause of the brain injuries found post mortem, so the police maintained. The incident was referred to as a scuffle.

Before the inquest, affidavits had been sworn by every person who had had any contact with Biko during his detention. Unfortunately for the police, none of these affidavits – twenty-eight of them in all – had made any mention of the alleged bump. Nor, it transpired from the evidence, had the three doctors who examined Biko while he was in detention ever been told of any bump on the head. The Security Police colonel in command in Port Elizabeth had not mentioned it either to the doctors or in his five affidavits.

Further, the bump on the head version was utterly destroyed by the expert medical evidence. Professor Proctor and Dr Gluckman expressed the firm opinion that the brain injuries suffered by Biko would have resulted in a period of unconsciousness of at least ten to twenty minutes. They were supported in their view by Professor Simson, head of the Department of Anatomical Pathology at the University of Pretoria. The state pathologist, Professor Laubser, did not dispute this. Yet the evidence of all the officers was that Biko fought, as one of them put it, like a wild animal throughout. Their evidence under cross-examination eliminated even the shortest period of unconsciousness.

Looking at these facts from what I hope is an objective distance, I have no doubt that between the evening of 6 September and the early morning of 7 September Steve Biko suffered a number of heavy blows to the head, inflicted by one or more of the security officers who had charge of him. This assault was probably carried out with some instrument which left no obvious external injury, such as – and here I guess – a sandbag or a loaded length of hosepipe, the latter object known from later evidence to have been used on other occasions by the Special Branch in Port Elizabeth.

Many years later, the major made an application for amnesty to the Truth and Reconciliation Commission. It was a strange application (ultimately rejected) because he did not admit to any misdeed. But he did describe his instructions given to him by his superiors regarding Biko. 'We should break him down in order to obtain information from him.' Steve Biko was hardly an easy man to break down. This was not his first experience of detention. One of his earlier spells of Special Branch detention had lasted 101 days, during which he had not yielded an inch to his interrogators. So the blows which caused his death were doubtless somebody's idea of breaking him down.

How was Steve Biko treated after he had received his injuries? He was stripped naked, his legs shackled and fixed to a grille, handcuffed for most of the time. He staggered, mumbled unintelligibly, did not take food or water, did not ask to go to the toilet, and was left lying on his urine-soaked blanket. The shackling and the nakedness were ordered by the colonel. When asked why he had given such orders, he replied that it was to prevent escape. When asked why, for decency's sake, this shackled man should not have been allowed to wear a pair of underpants, he replied that it was to prevent him from using them to commit suicide. This ludicrous answer was typical both of this officer's disregard for the truth and of his contempt for the most basic human rights of any person unfortunate enough to fall into his power.

It was obvious to this colonel that there was something seriously wrong with Biko. He therefore later on 7 September sent for the district surgeon. The district surgeon arrived and, after an examination, wrote out a certificate for the colonel. This doctor said in his evidence that he had noticed Biko's slurred speech and staggering gait. The possibility of a head injury had occurred to him, he said, but he asked no questions of either Biko or the colonel. The certificate he wrote out for the colonel stated simply that he could find no evidence of any abnormality or pathology on Mr Biko. He left him as he found him.

Why should an experienced district surgeon have been prepared to give such a misleading certificate? The answer became clear. The colonel had decided to take the line that Biko's slurred speech, his staggering, and his incontinence were shammed, to avoid interrogation, and he firmly turned the doctor's mind in that direction. He persisted even when the senior district surgeon, who was called in to examine Biko the next day, found a clinical sign that pointed strongly in the direction of neurological damage. The colonel still insisted that Biko was shamming even after a consulting physician who had been called in by the senior district surgeon carried out a lumbar puncture which showed blood cells in the spinal fluid. This pretence was kept up to the end.

The physician recommended that Biko be kept under close

observation in a hospital. The colonel refused to allow this. Instead, Biko was sent to the sick bay in a local prison, under the care of a medical orderly.

On the afternoon of 11 September he was found lying on the floor with froth on his mouth. He was described by the colonel himself as being in a semi-coma. At this late stage panic set in. The colonel remained unwilling to send him to a local hospital – for reasons which are not hard to guess – so it was decided to send him at once to Pretoria Central Prison. As no air ambulance was available, he was to be sent by road.

Steve Biko was placed on mats in the back of a Land Rover from which the rear seats had been removed. The captain whom I have already mentioned was in charge. The Land Rover was driven 700 miles through the night. There was no medical orderly with them. Biko was kept naked throughout the journey. According to the captain, that was to make it harder for him to escape. No medical reports were brought to Pretoria. Instead, the Pretoria officials were told falsely that the Port Elizabeth doctors had found nothing wrong with Mr Biko and that he was probably shamming. Yet the medical orderly at the Pretoria prison saw that he was seriously ill, and feared for his life.

That afternoon, on 12 September, Steve Biko died, lying on a mat in the Pretoria Prison Hospital. At the inquest we described it without, I think, any rhetorical exaggeration as a miserable and lonely death.

The verdict came on the morning after the inquest had ended, and contained no reasons. It took at most three minutes to deliver. The Chief Magistrate found that Stephen Bantu Biko had suffered extensive brain injuries, probably sustained during a scuffle with police officers on the morning of 7 September; and that the evidence did not prove that the death was brought about by any act involving or amounting to an offence on the part of any person.

So, once again, nobody was to blame. Given the history of previous inquests into deaths of detainees, the verdict, perverse as it was, was by no means a surprise to us. To quote Ecclesiastes, 'If thou seest the oppression of the poor and the violent perverting of judgment and justice in a province, marvel not at the matter'.

But many did marvel. The verdict caused outrage in South Africa and beyond. It flew in the face of all the evidence. Its formal result was to exonerate all the officers. They were not disciplined or even reprimanded for the manner in which they had treated Biko after he had sustained his injuries. On the contrary, the colonel was promoted to brigadier and so, in due course, was the captain.

In our closing address in the inquest court, we said this: 'Any verdict which can be seen as an exoneration of the Port Elizabeth Security Police will unfortunately be interpreted as a licence to abuse helpless people with impunity'. Unfortunately we were right. Over the following ten years more than thirty people died while in detention by the Security Branch or having passed through their hands.

So what do we take from this lamentable tale of the unpunished killing of a man of courage and of talents, a man of promise who might have become a man of destiny?

What of the inquest itself? It had shown us that there was indeed evil under the sun. It had at least exposed to the world and, more importantly, to many in South Africa whose eyes, ears, and hearts had been closed the cruelty and inhumanity inseparable from the regime of apartheid. It demonstrated that apartheid was not a social experiment which might or might not succeed, but was an exercise of power based only on force. This attitude of those who exercised that power was summed up in the comment of the minister on Biko's death and by the equally cold-hearted statements of the major and the colonel at the inquest. The major said that he felt bad about Biko's death because 'he was worth much more to us alive than dead'. The colonel said that he was upset when he learnt of Biko's death because 'it was a disaster for us that he could not be brought before a court and unmasked'.

The present South African Constitution has as its foundation the concept of 'ubuntu'. This word has been translated as 'a feeling of common humanity'. If a concept may be defined by its opposite, the feelings expressed by the minister, the major and the colonel are the exact opposite of ubuntu.

These events are far in the past. Under the new Constitution of South Africa such things do not happen. But it may still be worth considering how they could have happened under the old dispensation. The conduct which brought about the death of Steve Biko was of course completely unlawful. No statute permitted murder, assault, or deliberate medical neglect. There were laws which punished such things, there were courts and lawyers. So how could such things be done, and done with impunity?

If a simple answer is to be given, it is section 6 of the Terrorism Act 1967. The existing statutes had given ministers huge and draconian powers over individuals and communities.

But the difference in section 6 of the Terrorism Act was that it put absolute power directly into the hands of the police. That section authorised the police without judicial warrant to arrest and detain any person whom any senior police officer had reason to believe either had committed an offence under the act or had any knowledge of such offence. The object of the detention was interrogation, and there was no limit to the period of detention. The Act expressly provided that no court could order the release of a detainee. So habeas corpus was excluded. Moreover, a detainee was held incommunicado. He could not see or even write to a lawyer, a doctor of his own choice, or members of his own family. Sometimes reports of assaults on detainees leaked out, and applications for interdicts to stop abuse occasionally reached the courts. But the independence of the judiciary had been undermined by a policy of political appointments to the Bench. In all too many cases executive-minded judges sympathetic to the objectives of the government refused to intervene in cases concerning detainees, anxious only to ensure that court proceedings should not interfere with the interrogation process. Officers of the Security Branch who abused detainees knew that they had nothing to fear from their superiors, and little from legal proceedings. That is why, writing about Biko's death, Alan Paton could say:

> Any black who thinks that he has a right equal to the white man to move about South Africa freely, . . . and to share equally in its government, will end up in detention. But there is a possibility more grave than that, the possibility that he may die there.

Nor was it easy to publicise the treatment of detainees. During those years, the press was for the most part surprisingly free to criticise government action. However, the Nationalist government passed an Act which made it a criminal offence to publish any false statement about the police or about prisons unless the publisher could show that he had taken due care before publishing it. That may not sound unreasonable, but its practical effect was far-reaching. Even if a newspaper had a sworn statement from an ex-detainee alleging assault or torture, it could be sure that it would be disputed in court by the Security Branch officers concerned, with every chance that some equivalent of the Chief Magistrate of Pretoria would decide in their favour. As to taking due care before publishing, in the leading case under this statute the judge held that 'due care' required a newspaper to give the authorities advance notice of its proposed publication and await their comments. The chilling effect on the press was inevitable. The facts about the treatment of Steve Biko could be safely published only because they were disclosed in the inquest.

Now South Africa has a constitution with a comprehensive bill of rights which is enforced by the courts, and particularly by the Constitutional Court of South Africa – undoubtedly one of the great successes of the new constitution. This constitution and this court are admired throughout the democratic world. Seventeen years ago they established the rule of law in South Africa.

Nonetheless, a glance around the modern world shows us that nowhere can the rule of law be taken for granted. In the United States the two-hundred-year-old bill of rights has not prevented Guantanamo Bay. Even in the UK some politicians talk seriously about repealing the Human Rights Act. I do not claim any special political expertise, but my belief is that in modern constitutional democracies threats to the rule of law do not come so much from sweeping acts of legislation as from seemingly limited but incremental encroachments. I most certainly do not claim any qualification to comment on South African politics. However, as a lawyer who over a long – some would say too long – period has practised in different countries, I shall venture a few very general observations. It is a truism that a free, independent, and critical press is essential to the rule of law. So first I would say beware of any law which seeks to regulate the press. Statutory regulation, however reasonable it may look, will inevitably stifle both reporting and comment. The apartheid era press law is a clear example. It penalised only false statements and required of the press only reasonable care. But the actual result was censorship of reporting on police and prisons. Still more dangerous would be any extension of the Official Secrets Act beyond its traditional scope of protecting military secrets which could be of use to an enemy. Any more general definition of official secrets would inhibit legitimate investigative journalism. Wrongdoers should never be freed from the threat of exposure.

I would also beware of any measure which directly or even indirectly undermines the independence of the judiciary. Experience in many jurisdictions can show that this can take different forms. It might take the form of cutting down the jurisdiction of the courts. Or it might take the form of appointments to the Bench for political reasons or other reasons apart from merit. Diversity of the Bench is of real value, and merit may often be a matter of opinion, but the aim, even if not always attainable, should be to make merit the sole criterion for judicial appointment. As we saw under apartheid, a succession of political appointments undermines the respect for the judiciary as an institution.

It was famously said by one of the authors of the Constitution of the United States that the judiciary in its nature is the weakest branch of the government. Its power in the long run depends on its commanding the respect of society as a whole. The courts are rightly open to public criticism. Judgments of the courts may legitimately be subjected to strong criticism, even criticism which many of us would think unfair. Appointments to the Bench, like any other acts of government, must also be open to reasoned criticism. But scurrilous and ill-founded attacks on the integrity and motives of the courts as a whole or of individual judges undermine respect for the judiciary and so undermine the rule of law. Such attacks should be deprecated by all democrats and the motives of those who make them should be viewed with the utmost suspicion. They are particularly damaging when they come from persons within or close to government.

That is the end of my sermon. Let me return to Steve Biko.

After the inquest, I read some of his writings. I have recently re-read some of them. Even today, over thirty years on, in a radically changed society, their power is extraordinary. You find in them a combination of eloquence, insight, political passion, and political pragmatism. The Steve Biko Foundation, with the Director Mr Nkosinathi Biko, is to be congratulated for keeping alive not only his memory but also his principles. I shall try to say what I have taken from my reading.

Steve Biko's definition of Black Consciousness in the fewest words would be 'self-respect, pride in one's own people and culture, and, above all, self-reliance'. Blacks in South Africa, he asserted, must look to their own efforts to achieve freedom, not rely on the assistance of other groups. Blacks must never be complicit in their own oppression. He was quite uncompromising in this. He had hard words for those such as Kaiser Matanzima, who took office in the so-called Bantu homelands. As a student at the University of Natal he had been active in the National Union of South African Students, a body which was of course strongly opposed to apartheid, and whose white leaders had often attracted the attention of the Security Police. Yet in 1968 he led a breakaway of black students from NUSAS to form the South African Students Organisation. His writings at the time show that he had no ill-will towards NUSAS. His thinking was epitomised in the SASO slogan – 'Blackman, you are on your own'.

Much of his writing and speeches continued to be addressed to young people. His message, tough, uncompromising, and militant as it was, was entirely free of rancour or any expression of racism. Speaking immediately after his death, Bishop Desmond Tutu said that of all young blacks involved in working for change he was the least infected by racism. Here was a true principled and idealistic youth leader. It would be sad if such a man and what he stood for were to be forgotten.

Now much which Steve Biko lived and died for has come to pass, yet his words have not lost their relevance. His forthright analysis was that the struggle in South Africa was not a class struggle but a racial one. He said that on the one side was white racism and 'the antithesis to this must ipso facto be a strong solidarity amongst the blacks'. But out of these two situations he said one could hope to reach some kind of balance – 'a true humanity where power politics will have no place'. And he concluded one article in these words:

> Blacks have had enough experience as objects of racism not to wish to turn the tables. While it may be relevant now to talk about black in relation to white, we must not make it our preoccupation, for it can be a negative exercise . . .
>
> We have set out on a quest for true humanity, and somewhere on the distant horizon we can see the glittering prize . . . in time we shall be in a position to bestow upon South Africa the greatest gift possible – a more human face.

He did not live to see the end of that quest or to have that glittering prize within his grasp. He would, without doubt, have endorsed ubuntu as the foundation of a new South African constitution.

This evening we remember Stephen Bantu Biko – his life, a South African beacon, his death, a South African tragedy.

12

*A Barrister in the Apartheid Years**

~

I HAVE BEEN invited to speak to you about my time as an advocate in South Africa in the years of apartheid. Apartheid has gone forever. Why, then, speak of those dark years? Perhaps because it illuminates the place of the legal profession in maintaining the rule of law in any society, whether open or autocratic; and also the importance of an independent judiciary. It also presents a striking contrast to the present legal system in South Africa, and so underlines the value of a bill of rights and a judiciary able and willing to enforce it.

I shall speak mostly about cases in which I appeared. If you think that what is coming is the usual farrago of faulty recollection and self-serving anecdote which form the staple of lawyers' reminiscences, you will probably not be disappointed.

Let me start by defining apartheid. The main architect of the system was Dr Hendrik Verwoerd, as Prime Minister of South Africa. In the most nauseatingly hypocritical utterance of even that appalling man, he defined apartheid as meaning 'simply good neighbourliness'. What apartheid really meant was complete political and economic domination of blacks by whites. From the time that Europeans came to South Africa in 1652 there had always been racial prejudice and discrimination, but in the hands of the Nationalist party government after 1948 it became something of a different order. Racial discrimination was not merely permitted but required. Every citizen was classified according to race. There was compulsory racial segregation in residence and education. The government took powers to remove whole black communities

---

* This is a version of a talk given at the London School of Economics in 2002.

from their traditional areas to distant and desolate places without consent or compensation. A deliberately inferior system of education for blacks was introduced. And, of course, no blacks had the vote or a voice in making the laws by which they were governed. So far did the ideology of separation go that in the courts there were separate docks and separate witness boxes for white and black.

As blacks formed about four-fifths of the population of South Africa, it was obvious that these laws could never command general consent. To enforce them required a battery of coercive laws. The offence of terrorism was created with a frighteningly broad definition. There were heavy penalties for breaches of the segregation laws, but the ultimate weapon of the apartheid government was the power of the police without judicial warrant to arrest and detain any person for the purpose of interrogation. The detained person was held incommunicado, with no right to consult with a lawyer and no right to family or other visits. First the police were given powers to detain on this basis for ninety days; then it was increased to 180 days and, in due course, the detention could be (and often was) unlimited. Thus going to show again that all power is delightful and absolute power is absolutely delightful. At the same time, the power of the courts to grant habeas corpus was drastically curtailed.

Before 1948 the South African judiciary had a high reputation. After 1948 that reputation was somewhat tarnished by a series of blatant political appointments to the Bench: that is to say, appointments by the government of its political supporters, some of whom appeared to have no other qualification for high judicial office. Yet to a surprising degree the High Court bench maintained its independence. Some good judges were appointed, and even political appointees often disappointed the expectations of the government. A cynical former Minister of Justice was once heard to say that in his time he had made many political appointments to the Bench. The trouble with political appointments, he said, was that when they had been on the Bench for two weeks they imagined they had got there by merit. At all events, when acting for opponents of the government, one felt that one had at least a chance of winning, although it was often uphill work because of the draconian laws (often putting burdens of proof on accused persons) and because some of the judges were unable to overcome their political inclinations. I should add that there were no trials by jury: jury trials had disappeared – unlamented, because juries when they existed had consisted exclusively of white men.

There was, of course, no bill of rights in South Africa in those days. Such a thing was hardly conceivable in the days of apartheid. There was nothing which one could call a human rights bar. Many advocates whose general practices, like my own, covered a broad spectrum of civil and criminal cases found themselves drawn into political cases, that is to say, cases in which some politically motivated individual or group came into conflict with the apartheid laws and the security laws which backed them up. The clientele which fell into that category was remarkably varied. Apart from the really radical political activists, apartheid brought into conflict with the law people who would ordinarily not be classed as revolutionaries. I had among my clients standing in the dock in South Africa in criminal cases at least seven editors of leading South African newspapers, none radical and many conservative; also two professors of law, a leading Queen's Counsel and the Anglican Dean of Johannesburg, improbably charged with terrorism.

The dean, the Rev Gonville Aubie ffrench-Beytagh, was an interesting man. His field of expertise and interest was the ritual of the Church. He was not a political priest, but his detestation of the cruelties of apartheid had led him to establish a charitable fund to support the families of political prisoners on Robben Island. This aroused the ire of the government. Indeed, they probably thought his very name was an affront to them. At all events, they (or their security police) formed the view that his fund was a front for channelling money to banned African political organisations. This, if true, would have been an offence under the Terrorism Act, and the dean was accordingly charged with the crime of terrorism. The trial ran for two months. The prosecution witnesses were unimpressive and, fortunately, the books of the charity had been kept meticulously. Nonetheless, the judge, a notorious political appointee, found the dean guilty of terrorism and sentenced him to five years' imprisonment. The dean had been cross-examined for nearly eight days. The judge rejected his evidence.

A unanimous Appeal Court overturned the conviction. One of the advantages of trial by a judge alone rather than a jury is that a judge must give reasons for his findings, including his findings on the credibility of witnesses. The Appeal Court held that the judge's reasons for rejecting the defendant's evidence were wholly inadequate and unconvincing. A happy ending for the dean and for his worried counsel.

The dean was not my only ecclesiastical client. I seemed to specialise in them. The Bishop of Johannesburg instructed me to appear at the commission of inquiry into the fatal shootings by the police of 180 blacks at Sharpeville in 1960 on behalf of the black community there. There was Archbishop Desmond Tutu, to whom I shall refer again. I also appeared in defamation cases for a prominent black Lutheran bishop who had been grossly defamed by the wholly false accusation in a government-subsidised magazine that he had conspired to commit acts of violence. The judge awarded substantial damages to the bishop.

As for the political activists, I shall only mention three: Chief Albert Luthuli, a really great man, who was the President of the African National Congress in the 1950s; Nelson Mandela, who needs no description; and Archbishop Desmond Tutu, a theologian who felt compelled to speak for the black population because the major black political leaders of South Africa were either imprisoned or in exile. This leads me to say, without false or any other modesty, that I have one distinction which I doubt whether any other advocate can claim. All those three clients of mine were winners of the Nobel Peace Prize.

I acted for Nelson Mandela as junior counsel in the great treason trial of 1958 to 1961. One hundred and fifty leaders of the African National Congress and its allied movements had been arrested and charged with high treason. By the time the case came to trial in Pretoria at the end of 1958, various successful interlocutory applications had cut the number down to thirty. At the end of the trial in 1961, the panel of three judges (all of them nominated specifically for the trial by the Minister of Justice under a specific statutory power) unanimously acquitted all the accused. This acquittal was at the time a very remarkable event. It was after that trial that Nelson Mandela went underground. He was again arrested and tried for terrorism in 1964. There he was convicted. As the leader of the conspiracy to commit sabotage which had been found to exist, he was facing a possible sentence of death. In fact, as we all know, he was sentenced to life imprisonment. Thirty-one years later I was present when, as President of the Republic of South Africa, Nelson Mandela opened the first sitting of the new Constitutional Court in Johannesburg. He started by saying, with complete factual accuracy, 'The last time I entered a court of law it was to find out whether I was going to be sentenced to death'.

Was there an ethical problem in acting for the victims of the apartheid laws? One which was raised by critics of the legal profession rather than within the legal profession itself was of a very radical nature. These critics contended that those of us in the South African legal profession who acted for the defence in these political cases gave what they called 'a veneer of spurious respectability' to an unjust judicial system. In that way, they said, we were actually serving apartheid. Those critics were usually outside South Africa. They did not include the African National Congress. Perhaps there was some substance in their views. Under apartheid the judicial system had in some measure been corrupted. The corollary, according to the critics, was that we should somehow resign from this system, and certainly cease to act in political trials. I must confess that we advocates and attorneys in South Africa took little notice of these critics. We thought that the only ones who might be entitled to express such views were those at the sharp end, namely those who found themselves in the dock. Unsurprisingly, they took a very different view from the critics. They preferred acquittals, if they could get them, to convictions, even under an unjust system. And they preferred to have counsel to defend them.

There was one exceptional case. That was a case which came before a High Court judge in Natal. A number of young black men, political exiles, had come back into the country to commit sabotage. As so often happened, they walked straight into an ambush. Some of them made confessions; others, under duress, turned state evidence. Eight of them were charged with conspiracy to bomb a police station. This was a form of statutory terrorism where capital punishment was possible although not mandatory. These men refused to recognise the jurisdiction of what they called an apartheid court and they refused to have defence counsel. They refused, indeed, to take any part in the proceedings. Every morning they entered the court singing freedom songs. In the dock they talked and turned their backs on the judge. The exasperated judge from time to time made orders of committal for contempt – not much of a sanction, when the legislation provided for a minimum sentence of five years' imprisonment and a maximum sentence of death.

Not unexpectedly – the evidence was particularly strong – they were all convicted. They were sentenced to terms of imprisonment, save for one of them. The judge found that he was the ringleader of the conspiracy and sentenced him to death. The question for him then was whether he should appeal to the Appeal

Court, in his view an equally illegitimate tribunal. He decided he would. I was then briefed for him on the appeal. The record as I read it showed that he was far from being the ringleader of the conspiracy. As an Appeal Court judge later put it, he was a corporal rather than a captain. But what did appear was that he had been the ringleader of the contemptuous behaviour in court. Fortunately the Appeal Court saw it in the same way. The death penalty was hardly an appropriate sentence for contempt of court. They substituted a sentence of imprisonment. The austere critics no doubt considered that I should have refused to the brief and that my client should have persisted in his original attitude and refused to appeal, however stark the alternative.

One of the last cases I did in South Africa, in 1987, was another death sentence case. It was an appeal on behalf of six persons, including one woman, commonly known as the 'Sharpeville Six'. In the course of an anti-apartheid riot in a black township a black official had fled from his house pursued by a violent mob and then been killed in circumstances of revolting brutality. The actual killers were not found. The six accused were not alleged to have taken a direct part in the physical violence, but they were part of a large crowd of onlookers and, according to witnesses, they had been shouting encouragement to the killers. There was nothing to show that anything which they shouted had influenced the killers or even been heard by them. They were found guilty of murder on the basis that their vocal support showed that they had had a common purpose with the killers – entailing what some lawyers would consider an unprecedentedly broad application of the doctrine of common purpose. The trial judge described the killing, rightly, as a crime of medieval barbarity. He sentenced all of them to death.

As it happened, a stay of execution had been obtained from the court pending an application for leave to appeal only two days before they had been due to be executed. I had visited them on death row in Pretoria prison. If anyone still has any lingering affection for the death penalty, I would recommend a visit to death row. My clients – all persons of considerable fortitude – told me that the day before the stay was obtained each had been visited by the hangman. The visit was not social; it was to measure the circumference of their necks. I suggested to the Appeal Court, among other arguments, that to hang these six persons on the basis of the common purpose doctrine would also be a procedure of medieval barbarity. The appeal was wholly unsuccessful.

Although applications for clemency had previously been refused by
the State President, the six were eventually reprieved following
considerable diplomatic pressure, particularly from the United
Kingdom and Germany.

Let me finish this account of my cases with perhaps the
oddest case I was ever in. Under Emergency Powers legislation, the government had almost unlimited powers to declare a
state of emergency and to make regulations to deal with it. The
government was, of course, the sole judge of whether there was
an emergency, and its powers were freely used. At the time in
question there had been indeed a good deal of unrest at schools
in Soweto. Classes had been boycotted and there had been much
damage to school property. A regulation was made which created
an offence which I have not seen paralleled anywhere. In Soweto
it was made a crime for any schoolboy or girl to be outside his
or her classroom during school hours.

One morning a police major drove by a school. He saw a group of
children in the playground: they should have been in their classrooms. The police major drove off and came back with a squad of
police and some police lorries. Under the regulations, the police
major had great powers, including the power to detain not only
any person who committed an offence under the regulations, but
'any person if in his opinion it was necessary to do so to maintain
or restore law and order'. When the major returned to the school,
the children were still in the playground. He arrested all of them
and put them in the lorries. Not content with this, he sent his
men into the school to arrest those children who were in their
classrooms and all the teachers too. All the arrested children and
teachers were taken to police cells and locked up. Word soon got
round Soweto and solicitors were instructed to make a habeas
corpus application on behalf of the teachers and at least those
pupils who were arrested in the classrooms. The brief came to
me. This was one case which I could not lose. There could be no
grounds for arresting the children in school, still less the teachers.
It was a form of collective punishment. As I saw it, there was no
warrant for that even in the draconian regulations. If the major
had indeed formed the opinion that it was necessary to arrest
them, that opinion was irrational to the point of absurdity. You
may have heard of a nineteenth-century English Chancery judge
called Mr Justice Kekewich. It was said of him that before him no
case was certain and no case was hopeless. His family were said
to hold a day of rejoicing on the rare occasions that a judgment of

his was upheld by the Court of Appeal. I unhappily came before a judge who was the avatar of Mr Justice Kekewich. He could find nothing improper in the police conduct. The major had said on affidavit that he believed it necessary to arrest all those children and teachers for the maintenance of law and order, although he did not say why. The judge was not prepared to question his affidavit or his opinion. Our application was dismissed. The children and teachers were all released shortly afterwards, but they had learned their lesson – and, I fear, so had I.

I would like to turn now to a different aspect of legal practice in South Africa. In the period of which I have been speaking, there was either no state legal aid at all or (later) a wholly inadequate system. In 1978 there came a radical change in the legal landscape. In that year the Legal Resources Centre was founded by my wife Felicia, herself an advocate, and Arthur Chaskalson, also an advocate at the Johannesburg Bar. Arthur Chaskalson, a brilliant silk with a leading commercial practice, left the Bar to become full-time Director of the Centre. The Legal Resources Centre was a public interest law firm with a difference. It set out to take cases which would be test cases in the sense that, if successful, they would assist not only the individual litigant but large sections of the population. The method was to find and explore the chinks in the armour of the apartheid laws and in that way to establish hitherto unrecognised rights, particularly for the black population. The cases were carefully chosen, and presented by lawyers as good as any in the country. The courts proved to be surprisingly sympathetic.

Let me give you an example of the Legal Resources Centre's work under apartheid. The apartheid laws were designed to keep as many blacks as possible out of urban areas, and to expel as many as possible of those already there. The only blacks able to live in an urban area as a right, ie without a revocable permit, were those born there or those who had worked in the area continuously for ten years for the same employer. First, in the *Komani* case,[1] decided by the Appellate Division in 1981, the Legal Resources Centre succeeded in striking down a regulation which purported to prevent black men who were lawfully living in urban areas from having their wives and grown-up children

---

[1] *Komani NO v Bantu Affairs Administration Board, Peninsula Area* 1980(4) SA 448 (A).

living with them. Then, in the *Rikhoto* and *Mthiya* cases,[2] the
Legal Resources Centre attacked a typically ingenious and heart-
less official device which had been designed to prevent blacks from
taking advantage of the provision which gave them the right to
permanent residence after ten years' continuous employment with
the same employer. Regulations had been made which required
that black persons should be employed in urban areas only on
one-year contracts, which had to be renewed at the end of each
year. According to officialdom, ten annual contracts with the same
employer did not amount to ten years' continuous employment.
That ruling had never been challenged until the Legal Resources
Centre not only did so but persuaded the courts that the requirement of annual renewal did not prevent such employment being
continuous. Nor, contrary to the official view, did absence on long
leave. In the *Duma* case,[3] the Legal Resources Centre succeeded
in restricting the operation of the statute under which 'idle' blacks
could be deported from an urban area and sent to prison farms.
The government, the police and the lower courts had for years
worked on the convenient presumption (not contained in the
statute) that a black who had been unemployed for more than
three months in any year was deemed to be 'idle', however hard he
or she had tried to find work. The High Court, however, accepted
the submission of the Legal Resources Centre that 'idle' did not
bear the official meaning and meant nothing more or less than
idle in its ordinary sense.

This series of cases benefited literally hundreds of thousands of
blacks, who were for the first time held entitled to live lawfully
in cities and towns. Those victories were obtained in the courts
within the limits of the existing legal system.

The Legal Resources Centre naturally never had government
funding. It was funded by individuals and foundations in South
Africa, the United Kingdom, the United States of America, and
Europe.

I would draw two general lessons from the experience of the
Legal Resources Centre. First, it demonstrated to those oppressed
by apartheid that law could be a protection for the powerless and
not merely an instrument of domination.

The second lesson was that human rights should not be invoked
as the last resort in hopeless cases. Successful litigation in those

[2] *Oos-Randse Administrasieraad v Rikhoto* 1983(3) SA 595(A); *Mthiya v Black
Affairs Administration Board, Western Cape* 1983(3) SA 455 (C).
[3] *In re Duma* 1983(4) SA 469(N).

cases required solid research and, above all, an educated instinct for choosing the right issue, the right facts, and the right time to litigate.

That lesson remains.

POSTSCRIPT

After the demise of apartheid and to this day the Legal Resources Centre continues its work, now with the advantage of a legally enforceable bill of rights. Its first Director, Arthur Chaskalson, became the first President of the Constitutional Court and was later appointed Chief Justice of South Africa.